HOTSPOTS

MENO

Written by Tony Kelly, updated by Jane Egginton and Sasha Heseltine

Published by Thomas Cook Publishing
A division of Thomas Cook Tour Operations Limited.
Company registration no. 1450464 England
The Thomas Cook Business Park, Unit 9, Coningsby Road,
Peterborough PE3 8SB, United Kingdom
Email: books@thomascook.com, Tel: + 44 (0) 1733 416477
www.thomascookpublishing.com

Produced by Cambridge Publishing Management Limited
Burr Elm Court, Main Street, Caldecote CB23 7NU

ISBN: 978-1-84157-914-6

Series Editor: Diane Ashmore
Production/DTP: Steven Collins

Printed and bound in Italy by Printer Trento

CONTENTS

WHAT'S IN YOUR GUIDEBOOK?

Independent authors Impartial, up-to-date information from our travel experts who meticulously source local knowledge.

Experience Thomas Cook's 165 years in the travel industry and guidebook publishing enriches every word with expertise you can trust.

Travel know-how Contributions by thousands of staff around the globe, each one living and breathing travel.

Editors Travel-publishing professionals, pulling everything together to craft a perfect blend of words, pictures, maps and design.

You, the traveller We deliver a practical, no-nonsense approach to information, geared to how you really use it.

Explore the many charming alleys of Binibeca Vell

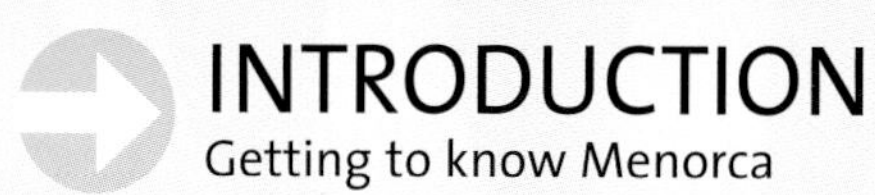

INTRODUCTION
Getting to know Menorca

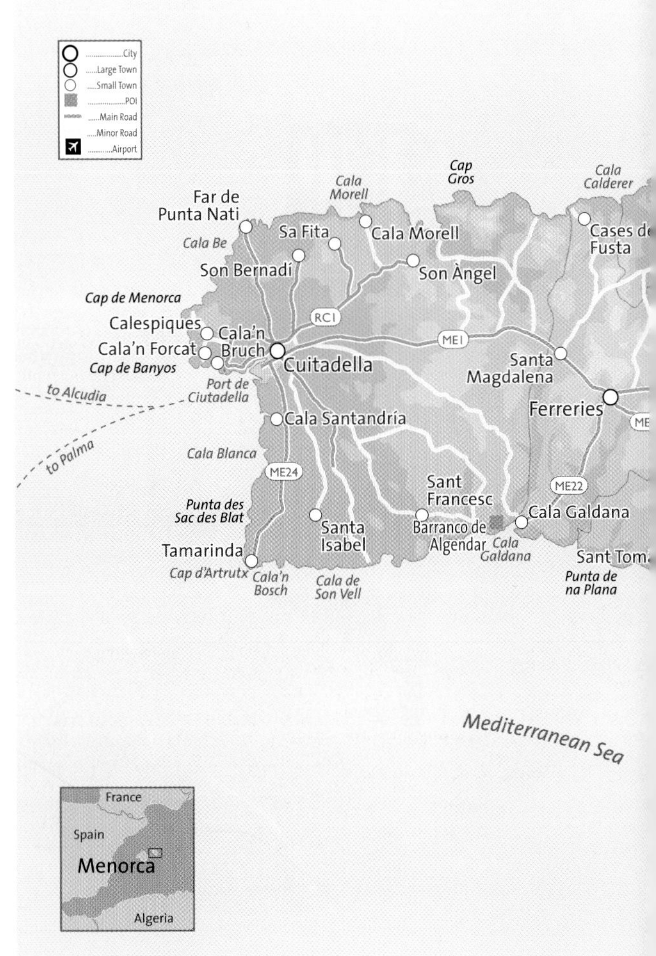
City
Large Town
Small Town
POI
Main Road
Minor Road
Airport
Cap Gros
Cala Morell
Cala Calderer
Far de Punta Nati
Sa Fita
Cala Morell
Cases de Fusta
Cala Be
Son Bernadí
Son Àngel
Cap de Menorca
RC1
Calespiques
Cala'n Bruch
ME1
Cala'n Forcat
Cuitadella
Santa Magdalena
Cap de Banyos
Port de Ciutadella
to Alcudia
Ferreries
Cala Santandría
to Palma
Cala Blanca
ME24
Sant Francesc
ME22
Punta des Sac des Blat
Cala Galdana
Santa Isabel
Barranco de Algendar
Cala Galdana
Tamarinda
Cap d'Artrutx
Cala'n Bosch
Cala de Son Vell
Punta de na Plana
Mediterranean Sea
France
Spain
Menorca
Algeria

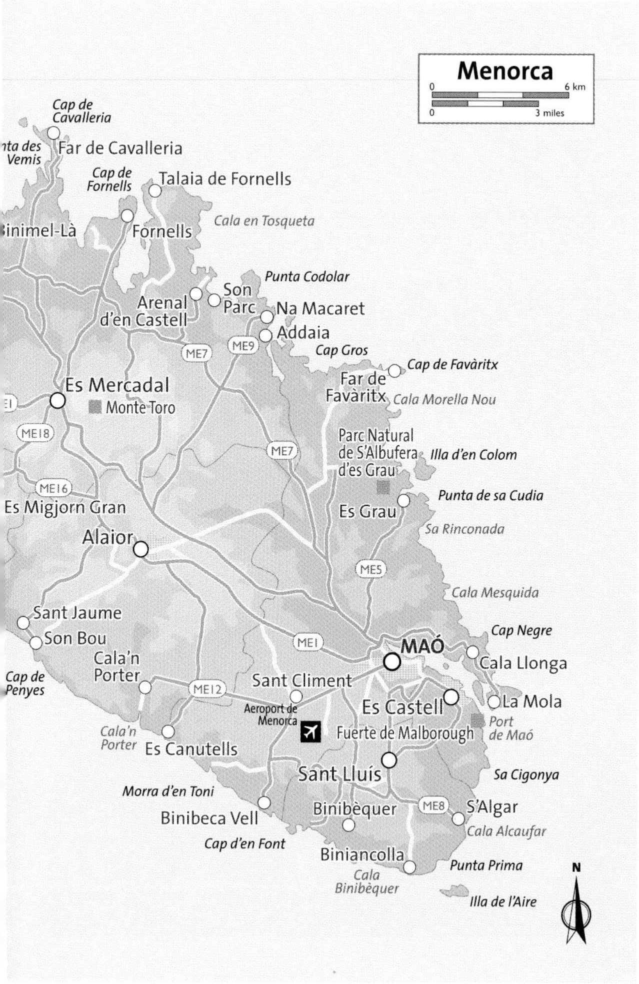
Menorca
0
6 km
0
3 miles
Cap de Cavalleria
Far de Cavalleria
Vemis
Cap de Fornells
Talaia de Fornells
Fornells
Cala en Tosqueta
Punta Codolar
Son Parc
Arenal d'en Castell
Na Macaret
Addaia
ME7
ME9
Cap Gros
Cap de Favàritx
Far de Favàritx
Cala Morella Nou
Es Mercadal
Monte Toro
ME18
ME7
Parc Natural de S'Albufera d'es Grau
Illa d'en Colom
ME16
Es Migjorn Gran
Punta de sa Cudia
Es Grau
Sa Rinconada
Alaior
ME5
Cala Mesquida
Sant Jaume
Son Bou
Cap Negre
ME1
MAÓ
Cala Llonga
Cala'n Porter
Cap de Penyes
ME12
Sant Climent
Aeroport de Menorca
Es Castell
La Mola
Port de Maó
Cala'n Porter
Es Canutells
Fuerte de Malborough
Sant Lluís
Sa Cigonya
Morra d'en Toni
Binibèquer
ME8
S'Algar
Binibeca Vell
Cala Alcaufar
Cap d'en Font
Biniancolla
Punta Prima
Cala Binibèquer
Illa de l'Aire
N

Maó's marina

Getting to know Menorca

Menorca is the second-largest of the Balearic islands. The largest island, Mallorca, is just 34 km (21 miles) away and the nearest city on the Spanish mainland is Barcelona, 225 km (140 miles) to the northwest.

Menorca's history goes back to the Talayotic period of around 2000 BC. Not much is known of the island's early inhabitants, but they left behind a wealth of prehistoric monuments, from watchtowers to burial caves. Later invaders left their mark too – the Romans introduced Christianity to the island and established a city at Maó (also known as Mahon), the Arabs introduced horses, still a Menorcan passion, and the Catalan conquest of 1287 opened the way for Menorca to become a part of modern Spain.

Menorca was ruled by the British for 70 years during the 18th century, and the British influence remains strong. The first British governor built a road across the island, moved the capital to Maó from Ciutadella, planted orchards and introduced new breeds of sheep and poultry.

Maó and Ciutadella are the main two cities. Maó, the modern capital, is a bustling city of businesses and government offices, with an old town of stylish shopping streets and one of the world's great harbours. Ciutadella, at the other end of the island, is much more traditional, with a Gothic cathedral and the palaces of the Catalan nobility, who refused to leave the city when the capital was moved to Maó. As a result, Ciutadella is the most Spanish place on Menorca, although it is now seeing an upsurge of sleek new restaurants and bars.

With its azure skies, endless sunshine and beaches of pale golden sand washed by a turquoise sea, Menorca has all the ingredients for a relaxing holiday. It has little of the hectic nightlife of Ibiza, although there is plenty of fun to be had after dark for those who seek it. Its beaches are some of the finest in Europe, from fun-packed family resorts to hidden pine-fringed coves. The peaceful countryside of rolling hills, meadows and dry-stone walls forms a gentle backdrop to the rocky coast, and the main towns at either end of the island are an intriguing mix of history, culture and style.

THE BEST OF MENORCA

TOP 10 ATTRACTIONS

- Wander the backstreets of **Maó** (see page 15), **Ferreries** (see page 81) and **Ciutadella** (see page 87), browsing in small, specialist shops among the shady alleyways.
- Visit **Maó's market** (see page 19) to taste Mahón cheese and buy a brightly patterned sarong, take a boat tour around **Es Port (Maó Harbour)** (see page 23), then look into the **Xoriguer distillery** on the waterfront to sample the local *pomada* (gin with lemon).
- Visit **Monte Toro** (see page 77), Menorca's highest point, to see the vast statue of Jesus and the tranquil convent.
- Try ***caldereta de langosta*** (lobster casserole) beside the harbour at **Fornells** (see page 64).
- Have a tapas lunch in **Ciutadella Harbour** (see pages 90–92) beneath the old city walls.

- Go to the **trotting races** (see page 29) in Maó at weekends and have a flutter.

- Learn about Menorca's history – complete with sound effects – at **Fuerte de Marlborough** (see page 24) near Es Castell.

- See the whitewashed 'fishing village' at **Binibeca Vell** (see page 32).

- Seek out some of Menorca's ancient monuments; the **Naveta d'es Tudons burial chamber** near Ciutadella (see page 88) or the **taulas of Torre Trencada**, worth the dusty ten-minute walk from the road.

- Watch the sun go down on the west coast at **Cap d'Artrutx** with Mallorca silhouetted on the horizon. Then watch the moon come up perched on the terrace at Cova d'en Xoroi nightclub in **Cala'n Porter** (see page 41).

Crystal-clear waters are perfect for snorkelling

SYMBOLS KEY

The following symbols are used throughout this book:

address telephone website address email

opening times important

The following symbols are used on the maps:

- information office
- post office
- shopping
- airport
- hospital
- police station
- bus station
- railway station
- church
- city
- large town
- small town
- POI (point of interest)
- motorway
- main road
- minor road
- railway
- numbers denote featured cafés, restaurants & evening venues

RESTAURANT CATEGORIES

The symbol after the name of each restaurant listed in this guide indicates the price of a typical three-course meal without drinks for one person:

£ budget price ££ mid-range price £££ most expensive

Menorca is an ideal family holiday destination

RESORTS

Places under the sun

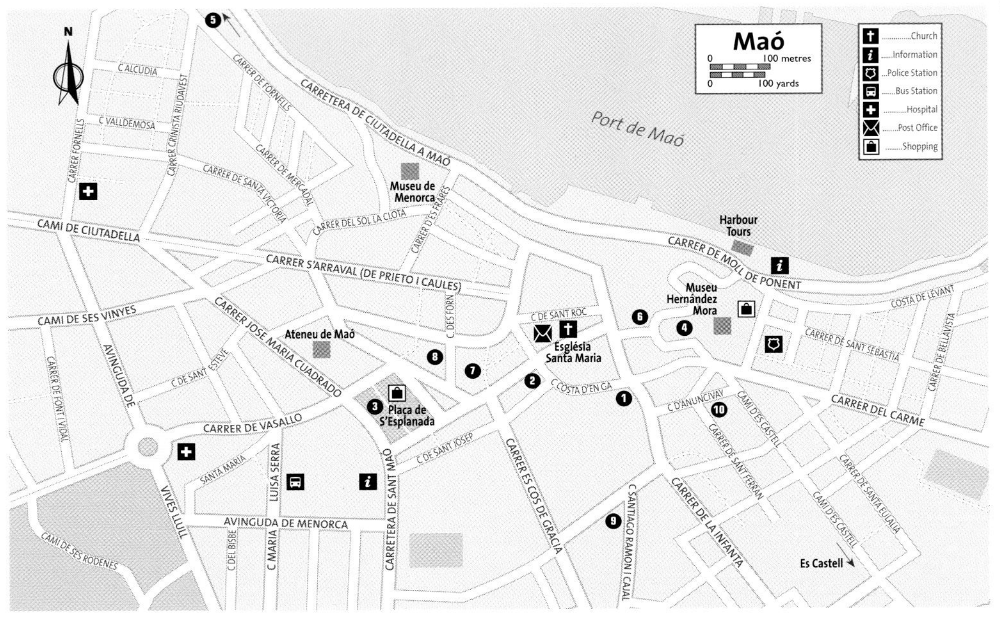
Maó
0 100 metres
0 100 yards
Church
Information
Police Station
Bus Station
Hospital
Post Office
Shopping
N
Port de Maó
Harbour Tours
CARRER DE MOLL DE PONENT
Museu Hernández Mora
Església Santa Maria
Museu de Menorca
Ateneu de Maó
Plaça de S'Esplanada
Es Castell
CARRETERA DE CIUTADELLA A MAÓ
CARRER DE FORNELLS
CARRER DE MERCADAL
CARRER DE SANTA VICTORIA
CARRER DEL SOL LA CLOTA
CARRER D'ES FRARES
C ALCUDIA
C VALLDEMOSA
CARRER CRINISTA RIUDAVEST
CARRER FORNELLS
CAMI DE CIUTADELLA
CARRER S'ARRAVAL (DE PRIETO I CAULES)
CAMI DE SES VINYES
CARRER JOSE MARIA CUADRADO
C. DES FORN
C DE SANT ROC
C DE SANT ESTEVE
AVINGUDA DE
CARRER DE FONT I VIDAL
CARRER DE VASALLO
SANTA MARIA
LUISA SERRA
AVINGUDA DE MENORCA
VIVES LLULL
CAMI DE SES RODENES
C DEL BISBE
C MARIA
CARRETERA DE SANT MAÓ
C DE SANT JOSEP
CARRER ES COS DE GRACIA
C COSTA D'EN GA
C SANTIAGO RAMON I CAJAL
C D'ANUNCIVAY
CAMI D'ES CASTELL
CARRER DE SANT FERRAN
CARRER DE LA INFANTA
CARRER DEL CARME
CARRER DE SANTA EULALIA
CARRER DE SANT SEBASTIÀ
COSTA DE LEVANT
CARRER DE BELLAVISTA

Maó

Founded in Roman times and rebuilt after the Catalan conquest, the city of Maó – also known as Mahón – reached its heyday when the first British governor, Sir Richard Kane, moved the capital here from Ciutadella in 1722 to utilise the vast natural harbour. You can still feel the British influence today in streets like Carrer Isabel II, where fine Georgian terraced houses feature sash windows.

Maó (pronounced 'Ma-oh') is a city for leisurely strolling along the pedestrian shopping streets of the old town, which tumble down the hill from the main square, Plaça de S'Esplanada, to the port. Wander down any side streets and you come across hidden alleys, stylish shops or an unexpected glimpse of an ancient archway, the only surviving section of the old city walls.

Plaça de S'Esplanada is the city's meeting place, where children play and old men sit beneath the trees while the bustling life of a modern capital goes on around them – the best place to watch it all happening is from one of the cafés that line the square.

THINGS TO SEE & DO

Ateneu de Maó (Natural History Museum)

This local museum has magnificent cabinets of stuffed seabirds, spiny crabs and lobsters, and fossils.

ⓐ Conte de Cifuentes 25 ⓣ 971 36 05 53 ⓦ www.ateneumao.org
ⓛ 10.00–14.00 & 17.30–22.00 Mon–Fri, 10.00–14.00 Sat

Maó, or Mahón as it is often called, gave mayonnaise to the world. The word was invented by the French Duke of Richelieu, who used mayo as an aphrodisiac – mahonesa translates as 'a girl from Mahón'!

Església Santa Maria (St Mary's church)

The highlight of Maó's biggest church is its Swiss organ, with more than 3,000 pipes. Organ concerts are given from April to October at 11.30 every morning except Sundays.

ⓐ Plaça de Sa Constitució 🕒 08.00–13.00 & 18.00–20.30

Museu Hernández Mora

This museum has a fascinating collection of island maps bequeathed by a local author.

ⓐ Claustre del Carme ⓣ 971 35 05 97 ⓦ www.ajmao.org 🕒 10.00–13.00 Mon–Sat

Museu de Menorca

At the time of writing, this museum was under messy renovation but still open. It is in the cloisters of the former Franciscan convent and

Beneath the city walls in Maó

S'Albufera d'es Grau

contains finds from the Bronze Age sites across Menorca as well as paintings from the 18th century, when the British still ruled.
Ⓐ Avinguda Doctor Guàrdia Ⓣ 971 35 09 55 Ⓛ 10.00–14.00 & 18.00–20.30 Tues–Sat, 10.00–14.00 Sun (Apr–Oct); 09.30–14.00 Tues–Fri, 10.00–14.00 Sat & Sun (Nov–Mar) ⓘ Closed Mon

EXCURSION

Parc Naturel de S'Albufera d'es Grau

This beautiful natural park, centred on a massive lagoon halfway between Arenal d'en Castell and Maó, is a paradise for walkers, bird-watchers and nature-lovers. The park is currently subject to a massive conservation programme which will see the regrowth of indigenous flora. Leave the car behind, don your walking shoes, take plenty of drinking water to trek the well-marked walking trails, and look out for tree frogs, lizards, aquatic terrapins, booted eagles and brightly coloured bee-eaters on the way. The long, sandy beach at Es Grau is ideal

for children, sloping gently into the clear, shallow water. Boat excursions can be arranged to the Illa d'en Colom, Menorca's largest offshore island, named after a notorious pirate.
ⓐ Centro de Recepción Rodríguez Femenias, Carretera de Maó es Grau Km 3.5, Llimpa ⓣ 971 35 63 02 ⓛ 09.00–18.00 Wed–Sat, 09.00–15.00 Sun (summer); 09.00–15.00 Wed–Sun (winter)

TAKING A BREAK

Restaurants & bars

Although some of Maó's best restaurants are by the waterfront on the road around the harbour, there are some great eating places in the city centre and around.

American Bar £ ❶ A perfect place to watch the world go by under an art deco sign. The square outside is a popular meeting place for local families at the weekend. ⓐ Plaça Reial 1 ⓣ 971 36 31 83 ⓛ 07.00–22.00 Tues–Sun

Café I Gelats Parpal £ ❷ An odd cross between a shop selling wooden models of boats, a bar-café serving copious piles of paella at reasonable prices, and an internet café called World Next Door. Good value for the centre of Maó and always busy. ⓐ Carrer Hannover 21 ⓣ 971 35 34 75 ⓛ 11.00–22.00

J & J Fish & Chips £ ❸ Traditional English fish and chips to take away or eat on the terrace; right in the middle of all the action on market days. ⓐ Plaça de S'Esplanada ⓣ 971 36 94 13 ⓛ 11.00–16.00 Mon, Tues & Sat, 11.00–16.00, 18.30–21.00 Wed–Fri

Mirador Café £ ❹ This buzzing café, on the ramparts overlooking the harbour, attracts a young and noisy crowd singing along to British pop. Bar snacks include filled rolls and unusual salads. ⓐ Plaça Espanya 2 ⓛ 10.00–01.00 Mon–Sat

SHOPPING

Llibreria Fundació is a good bookshop for maps and books on Menorca, and copies of the local English-language magazine *Roqueta* (Carrer Hannover 14 09.30–13.30 & 17.00–20.00 Closed Sat afternoon & Sun).

Try **Sucreria Vallès** (Carrer Hannover 19) for cakes, handmade chocolates and giant *ensaimadas* (light, fluffy buns dusted with icing sugar), and the long-established **El Turronero** confectioners (Carrer Nou 22–26), for delicious nougat, sugared almonds and toffee, lemon and meringue-flavoured ice creams. **Colmado La Palma** (Carrer Hannover 15) is a deli and off-licence selling salamis, local Es Canyis cheese and Xoriguer gins and liqueurs.

Market Maó's covered market is beautifully situated in elegant cloisters next door to the Carmelite church (Mon–Sat, mornings only). This is the best place to pick up Mahón cheese, cured ham and several varieties of Menorcan pork sausages. The fish market is in a separate building up the road.

The Old Town

The streets between Plaça de S'Esplanada and the market are the areas to search out Maó's most stylish boutiques and galleries. For good leather bags and shoes, look out for the local branch of **Jaime Mascaro** or **Looky** in Carrer Ses Moreres. **M&Ms** at the top of Carrer Hannover has stunning and stunningly expensive jewellery, leather goods and designer housewares.

Add a touch of glitz to your life with **La Perla** and **D&G** underwear from **Glamour** (Carrer Bastió 39). Well-known international brands include **Mango** (S'Arravaleta) for Spanish fashions, and a branch of the **Body Shop** in Carrer Nou.

Supermarkets

There are various supermarkets on the outskirts of Maó and in Sant Lluís. Most open 09.00–21.00 Mon–Sat; some open 09.00–14.00 Sun.

Bar Restaurant Tamarindos ££ ❺ Watch the sun disappear over a platter of prawns perched by the sea in Es Grau. One for really kicking back! ⓐ Pas des Tamarrells 14, Es Grau ⓣ 971 35 94 20 ⓛ 12.00–16.00 & 17.00–22.30

Café and Delicatessen Can Pota ££ ❻ One of a new generation of tapas bars, this is on the corner of Carrer de Ses Voltes overlooking the harbour. Snaffle top-notch tapas at the zinc bar perched on a designer stool. Afterwards buy expensive olive oils, Menorcan gins and turron to take home with you. ⓐ Portal de Mar 11 ⓣ 971 36 23 63 ⓛ 12.00–15.00 & 17.00–22.30 Mon–Sat

▲ *Maó harbour seen from the town*

La Tropical ££ ❼ There are only a few outdoor tables under an awning just off busy Carrer Ses Moreres, but this tiny Spanish restaurant serves some of the freshest fish in town. Try the 'menu from the market', which changes daily. ⓐ Carrer de sa Lluna 36 ⓣ 971 36 05 56 ⓒ 13.00–16.00 & 19.30–24.00

Antiga Casa Pilar £££ ❽ This is more like eating in a private home than a restaurant – top-quality Mediterranean cooking tucked away in a backstreet house with a garden terrace. Expensive, but really worth it. ⓐ Carrer des Forn 61 ⓣ 971 36 68 17 ⓒ 13.00–15.30 ⓘ Booking required

AFTER DARK

Maó's nightlife is centred on the waterfront at Moll de Ponent, but there are now some really happening nightspots in town.

Bars & clubs

Café Blues £ ❾ Trendy basement bar, playing mostly jazz and blues. ⓐ Carrer Santiago Ramon i Cajal 3 ⓒ 19.00–late Tues–Sun

Vineria Parra £ ❿ Currently the coolest call in town, with reggae, funk and hip-hop nights plus art exhibitions. There is internet access too. The kitchen is open until 00.30. ⓐ Carrer Sant Ferran 3 ⓣ 971 36 36 36 ⓒ 20.00–03.00 Wed–Sun

> It can be tricky to find a parking space at street level in Maó's city centre, especially when the market is on in Plaça de S'Esplanada. Your best bet is to use the underground car parks under Plaça de S'Esplanada or along Es Cos de Gracia, on the opposite side of the road and a little further on from the tourist information centre. Failing that, come into town by bus, or drive down to the harbour where there is usually more parking space.

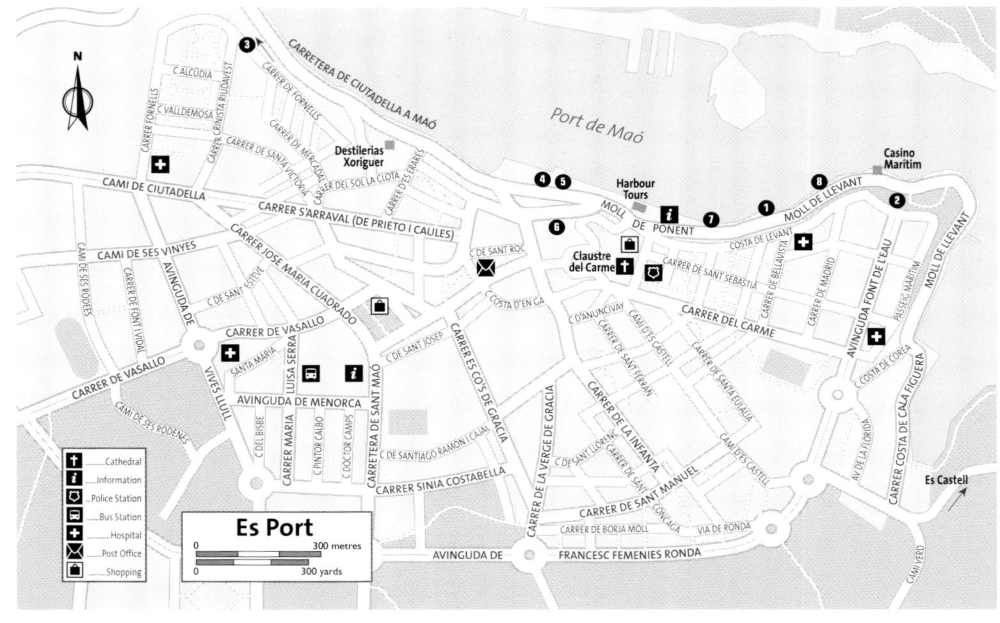
N
Port de Maó
CARRETERA DE CIUTADELLA A MAÓ
Destilerias Xoriguer
Harbour Tours
Casino Marítim
Claustre del Carme
Es Castell
MOLL DE PONENT
MOLL DE LLEVANT
PASSEIG MARITIM
AVINGUDA FONT DE L'EAU
CARRER COSTA DE CALA FIGUERA
C COSTA DE COREA
AV DE LA FLORIDA
CAMI VERD
CARRER DE MADRID
CARRER DE BELLAVISTA
COSTA DE LEVANT
CARRER DE SANT SEBASTIA
CARRER DEL CARME
CARRER DE SANTA EULALIA
CAMI D'ES CASTELL
CARRER DE SANT FERRAN
C D'ANUNCIVAY
CARRER DE LA INFANTA
C DE SANT LLORENC
CARRER DE SANT
CARRER DE SANT MANUEL
CONCAGA
VIA DE RONDA
CARRER DE BORJA MOLL
AVINGUDA DE
FRANCESC FEMENIES RONDA
CARRER DE LA VERGE DE GRACIA
CARRER ES CO'S DE GRACIA
C COSTA D'EN GA
C DE SANT ROC
CARRER SINIA COSTABELLA
C DE SANTIAGO RAMON I CAJAL
C DE SANT JOSEP
CARRETERA DE SANT MAÓ
C DOCTOR CAMPS
C PINTOR CALBO
CARRER MARIA
C DEL BISBE
AVINGUDA DE MENORCA
LUISA SERRA
SANTA MARIA
CARRER JOSE MARIA CUADRADO
C DE SANT ESTEVE
CARRER DE VASALLO
AVINGUDA DE
VIVES LLULL
CAMI DE SES RODENES
CARRER S'ARRAVAL (DE PRIETO I CAULES)
CARRER D'ES ERARES
CARRER DEL SOL LA CLOTA
CARRER DE MERCADAL
CARRER DE SANTA VICTORIA
CARRER DE FORNELLS
CARRER CRINISTA RIUDAVEST
C ALCUDIA
C VALLDEMOSA
CARRER FORNELLS
CAMI DE CIUTADELLA
CAMI DE SES VINYES
CARRER DE FONT I VIDAL
CAMI DE SES RODEES
1
2
3
4
5
6
7
8
Cathedral
Information
Police Station
Bus Station
Hospital
Post Office
Shopping
Es Port
0
300 metres
0
300 yards

Es Port (Maó Harbour) & Es Castell (the Castle)

Maó Harbour, known as Es Port, is 5 km (3 miles) long and 1 km (⅔ mile) across at its widest point, and is one of the largest natural deep-water ports in the world after Pearl Harbor. Due to this fact, and its location in the Mediterranean, Maó has been a strategic stronghold for many nations throughout history.

The best way to see the harbour at sea level is to join one of the boat tours that leave regularly from both Maó and Es Castell, which sits southeast of Maó at the harbour mouth. The guides point out the famous buildings lining the banks such as Golden Farm, the plum-red Georgian mansion high on the northern shore where Lord Nelson, the British admiral, may have stayed with his mistress Lady Hamilton. Out in the harbour are three islands: the first, Illa del Rei (King's Island), is where King Alfonso III landed in 1287 to capture Menorca from the Moors. The British later built a hospital for sick sailors there and renamed it Bloody Island. Further out, boats were placed under quarantine on Illa Plana (Flat Island) until Illa de Llatzeret (the name derives from Lazarus in the Bible, and the islet was known as Quarantine Island by the British) was built in the 1810s. Further down the harbour still, the great fortress of La Mola was built to protect the port and later gained notoriety for housing political prisoners.

On the southeast side of the harbour is the old British garrison town of Es Castell, the most easterly town in Spain. Previously known as Villacarlos by the Spanish and Georgetown by the British, it contains many Georgian buildings – especially around the main square, Plaça de S'Esplanada. One of the former barracks contains an interesting military museum (ⓐ Plaça de S'Esplanada ⓑ 11.00–13.00 Sat & Sun). The harbour at Cales Fonts in Es Castell is perfectly placed to catch the afternoon sun and people flock here to eat at the water-side restaurants.

BEACHES

There are no beaches in Maó Harbour. The nearest is at **Cala Mesquida**, signposted from the road between Maó and La Mola.

THINGS TO SEE & DO

Casino Marítim

Play roulette, blackjack and poker in plush surroundings overlooking the port. There's a cocktail bar and a swish restaurant too.
Ⓐ Moll de Llevant 287 Ⓣ 971 36 49 62 Ⓦ www.casinomaritimo.es
Ⓛ 09.00–05.00

Destilerias Xoriguer

Gin was the drink of choice among British sailors stationed in Mahón in the 16th and 17th centuries so entrepreneurial Menorcans set about making their own version. The result was Xoriguer, still run as a family business. Visit the distillery on the waterfront to see the old-fashioned copper stills and taste a wide range of gin-based products.
Ⓐ Moll de Ponent 91 Ⓣ 971 36 21 97 Ⓦ www.xoriguer.es Ⓛ 08.00–19.00 Mon–Fri, 09.00–13.00 Sat Ⓘ Admission charge

Fuerte de Marlborough

This massive fortress built by the British between 1710 and 1726, near the entrance to Maó Harbour at picturesque Cala Sant Esteve, has a Martello tower and a network of underground tunnels. It was named after Sir John Churchill, Duke of Marlborough.
Ⓐ Cala Sant Esteve Ⓣ 971 36 04 62 Ⓛ 09.00–13.00 & 15.00–19.00 Tues–Sat, 09.30–13.00 Sun Ⓘ Admission charge

Harbour tours

These leave frequently from Maó waterfront at the bottom of Carrer de Ses Voltes and from Cales Fonts in Es Castell. Some of the tours use glass-bottomed boats, so you can see fish swimming underwater.

Maó Harbour has been strategically important throughout history

TAKING A BREAK IN ES PORT (MAÓ HARBOUR)

The restaurants stretch along the harbour fronts of Maó (see map on page 22). They serve local Menorcan cuisine, Italian, Indian and Chinese.

Sa Taverna d'Es Port £ ❶ A down-to-earth tapas bar with a wide selection of meatballs, seafood and salads. Unbelievable value considering its position along the harbour side. Ⓐ Moll de Llevant 115 Ⓣ 971 36 79 09 Ⓛ 12.00–15.00 & 20.00–23.00

Roma ££ ❷ Popular restaurant beside the moorings, with dining space underneath awnings. It's always crowded with families lapping up huge plates of spaghetti Bolognese and crispy pizza, and it's great value for money. Ⓐ Moll de Llevant 295 Ⓣ 971 35 37 77 Ⓛ 12.30–24.00

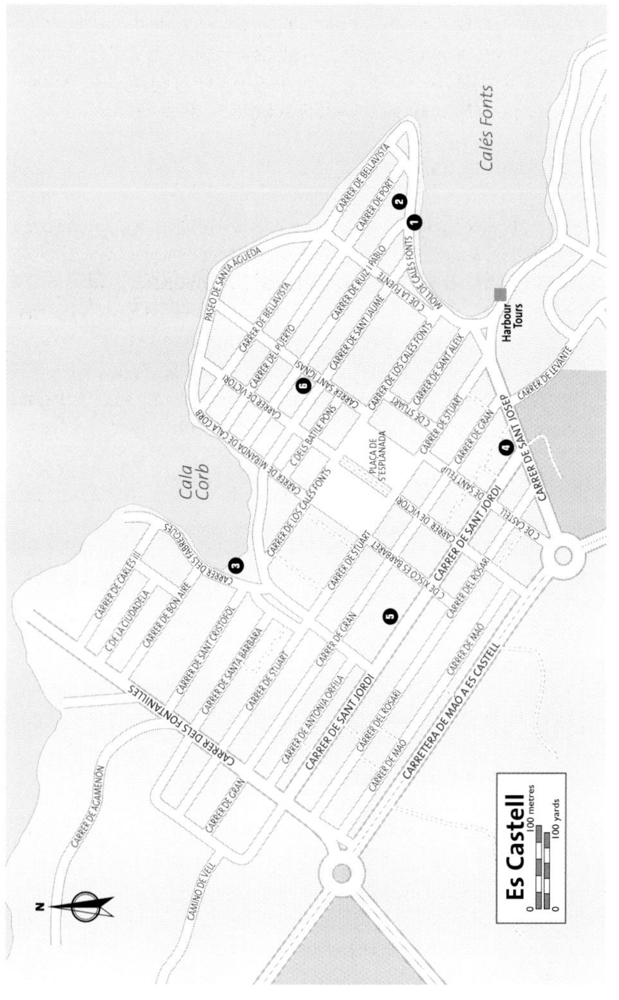
Es Castell
0
100 metres
0
100 yards
N
Calés Fonts
Cala Corb
Harbour Tours
PLAÇA DE S'ESPLANADA
CARRER DE BELLAVISTA
CARRER DE PORT
MOLL DE CALES FONTS
CARRER DE RUIZ I PABLO
C DE LA FUENTE
PASEO DE SANTA AGUEDA
CARRER DEL PUERTO
CARRER DE SANT JAUME
CARRER DE LOS CALES FONTS
CARRER DE SANT ALEIX
CARRER SANT IGNASI
CARRER DE VICTORI
CARRER DE MIRANDA DE CALA CORB
C DELS BATLLE PONS
C DE STUART
CARRER DE STUART
CARRER DE GRAN
CARRER DE SANT JOSEP
CARRER DE LEVANTE
DE SANT FELIP
C DE CASTELL
CARRER DE SANT JORDI
CARRER DEL ROSARI
C DE XISCO ES BARBARET
CARRER DELS FABREGUES
CARRER DE CARLES III
C DE LA CIUDADELA
CARRER DE BON AIRE
CARRER DE SANT CRISTOFOL
CARRER DE SANTA BARBARA
CARRER DE ANTONIA ORFILA
CARRER DE MAÓ
CARRETERA DE MAÓ A ES CASTELL
CARRER DELS FONTANILLES
CARRER DE AGAMENON
CAMINO DE VELL
1
2
3
4
5
6

Es Cap Roig £££ ❸ Splash out on quality seafood served in a romantic setting with views over the cliffs to cute Cala Mesquida. Booking is vital for the evening. ⓐ Contra Cala Mesquida ⓣ 971 18 83 83 ⓛ 12.00–16.00 & 19.00–24.00 ⓘ Booking advised; closed Mon lunchtime

AFTER DARK IN ES PORT

The area at the foot of the harbour steps in Maó is a busy late-night meeting place with several fashionable bars. Along Moll de Ponent you'll find **Club Akelarre Jazz** ❹ for late-night concerts (No 41) and **Pub Salsa** ❺ for Latino sounds (No 290), or **Berri** ❻ (Costes des Generales) for funky music and bopping Spaniards. Saloon-bar-style **Bar Texas** ❼ (ⓐ Moll de Llevant 65) has rowdy singing and dancing on tables until well past 24.00, while smooth **Mambo** ❽ (ⓐ Moll de Llevant 209) is packed with smartly dressed locals doing their thing at the late-night cocktail bar with a pretty terrace.

TAKING A BREAK IN ES CASTELL (THE CASTLE)

Ca'n Delio ££ ❶ What could be more romantic than fresh sardines and chilled wine beside the sea on a summer evening? Alternatively, splash out on lobster *caldereta* for a long family lunch. ⓐ Moll de Cales Fonts 38 ⓣ 971 35 17 11 ⓛ 12.30–15.30 & 19.00–24.00

El Trebol ££ ❷ Sample the best fish in town as the sun goes down. ⓐ Moll de Cales Fonts 43 ⓣ 971 36 70 97 ⓛ 12.30–15.30 & 19.30–23.00

AFTER DARK IN ES CASTELL

Local musicians gather at **Es Cau** ❸, a bar set inside a fishermen's cave in the tiny harbour of Cala Corb (ⓐ Carrer Fabregues). For a more refined atmosphere, try the **Piano Bar** ❹ (ⓐ Carrer Sant Ignasi 11) or **Colibri** ❺ music bar (ⓐ Sant Josep 45b). The disco pub **Mamas & Papas** ❻ (ⓐ Sant Jordí 10-A) attracts a lively late-night crowd, with karaoke from 23.00–04.00.

S'Algar, Cala Alcaufar & Punta Prima

The stretch of rocky coastline running along Menorca's southeastern shore is indented with pretty coves. There are few high-rise buildings and much of the area is still wild. This is where you will find some of Menorca's most peaceful and stylish resorts, including S'Algar, Cala Alcaufar and Punta Prima.

Purpose-built S'Algar (pronounced 'Sal-gar') possesses some of the best sporting facilities on the island and a mini-train for the children but no beach, although there is a minute cove with rock bathing. Nearby Cala Alcaufar (pronounced 'Alco-far') is a tiny, relaxing resort, once a fishing village and now ideal for enjoying the peace and tranquillity of rural Menorca. Punta Prima, at the island's southeastern tip, was appropriately

The peaceful resort of S'Algar

named Sandy Bay by the British during their domination of the island. The resort here has long been a popular holiday spot among Menorcans.

Just inland from the coast is Sant Lluís, a dazzling village of whitewashed houses founded by the French in 1756. In the surrounding countryside, you can still see some of the ancient farmhouses that once surrounded the village.

BEACHES

The largest beach in southeastern Menorca is at Punta Prima, looking across to the tiny island of Illa de l'Aire, uninhabited except for a rare species of black lizard. The lovely sandy beach that gently shelves into the crystal-clear waters of the pretty, cliff-lined bay at Cala Alcaufar makes it a popular choice for families and non-swimmers. Both beaches have sunbeds and parasols for hire, and there are pedaloes at Punta Prima.

THINGS TO SEE & DO

Cala Rafalet

Take a walk down the thickly wooded gorge to the tiny inlet beach at Cala Rafalet in S'Algar for peace and quiet and some excellent snorkelling.

Hipódrom Municipal de Maó (Maó's Hippodrome)

Maó's racetrack is situated just outside Sant Lluís, and popular trotting races are held on Saturday evenings at around 17.30.

ⓐ Avinguda JA Clavé 400 ⓣ 971 36 86 62 ⓦ www.hipodromdemao.com
◷ From 17.30 Sat

Molí de Dalt

This restored windmill with a conical blue-and-white roof is now a museum with a collection of old farming and milling tools.

ⓐ Carretera Sant Lluís 4 ⓣ 971 15 10 84 ◷ 10.00–14.00, 17.00–20.00 Mon–Sat, 11.00–13.00 Sun

S'Algar Sports

An extensive complex offering a wide range of sports from mountain biking, sailing and kayaking to tennis, mini-golf, archery and bowls. ⓐ Club Hotel San Luís ⓣ 971 35 94 54 ◷ 10.00–13.00 ⓘ Daily Children's Club called S'Algui ◷ 10.00–13.00 & 15.00–17.30 ⓘ You must reserve activities 24 hours in advance at the information desk opposite La Raqueta café

Watersports

Try your hand at diving, water-skiing or sailing at S'Algar Diving Menorca. There are also scuba trips and tuition as well as snorkelling expeditions. ⓐ S'Algar Diving Menorca, Passeig Marítim, S'Algar, Sant Lluís ⓣ 971 15 06 10 ⓦ www.salgardiving.com

TAKING A BREAK

Restaurants

Sebastian Place £ Popular bar with satellite TV, a pool table, lots of teenagers, and live music most nights. Occasionally there is rowdy organ music, popular with the Menorcans at the weekends. ⓐ Carrer Mayosu, Punta Prima ⓣ 971 15 90 68 ◷ 10.00–02.00

Asia ££ One of several restaurants in the Hotel San Luís boasting one of the very few decent Asian menus on the island. A refreshing change from paella! ⓐ Urbanización S'Algar, S'Algar ⓣ 971 35 94 54 ⓦ www.salgarhotels.com ◷ 19.00–23.00

La Rueda ££ Busy village restaurant (upstairs) serving Galician delicacies and tapas bar on the main street of Sant Lluís. The locals come here to eat fried squid rings, octopus and meatballs in tomato sauce. ⓐ Carrer Sant Lluís 30, Sant Lluís ⓣ 971 15 03 49 ◷ 12.30–15.30 & 19.30–23.30 Wed–Mon (restaurant); 06.30–24.00 Wed–Mon (bar)

Pan y Vino £££ Stylish British-run restaurant in a 200-year-old farmhouse in the hamlet of Torret, near Sant Lluís. Great modern cooking with the

Molí de Dalt

very best local ingredients; you'll often spot a famous face dining here! Camí de la Coixa 3, Torret 971 15 03 22 www.panyvinomenorca.com 20.00–23.00 Sat–Wed (June–Sept) Booking essential

La Venta de Paco £££ Excellent traditional Menorcan restaurant opposite the roundabout as you drive into the village from Maó. Go native with suckling pig and barbecued goat. Avinguda Sa Pau 158, Sant Lluís 971 15 07 93 12.30–16.00 & 19.00–24.00 Closed Mon

AFTER DARK

This is a quiet stretch of coastline, although both the S'Algar Hotel and the Club Hotel San Luis in S'Algar have discos (early evenings are for the children!). With the exception of Sebastian Place (see opposite), most other venues close before 23.00.

Binibeca Vell

The rocky coast from Binibeca to Es Canutells boasts some of Menorca's finest seascapes with small, sandy beaches lined with attractive holiday resorts. The star attraction is undoubtedly Binibeca Vell, with an award-winning, Moorish-style complex designed as a modern fishing village.

The development attracted international attention when it was designed by Spanish architect Antonio Sintes in 1972. Until then, Menorca's tourist resorts had consisted mostly of high-rise hotels, but Binibeca was consciously different – a dazzling maze of whitewashed cottages with wooden balconies tumbling down narrow alleyways to a small fishing harbour.

A short walk to the east brings you to the neighbouring resorts of Binibeca Nou and Cala Torret. To the north is the quiet little backwater of Binisafua, with its tiny beach at the end of a pretty inlet.

BEACHES

Binibeca beach, between Binibeca Vell and Cala Torret, has shallow water and clean sand, making it popular with families and safe for swimming. From the car park, a path leads through the pine trees to a shaded picnic area in the cove.

Binibeca Vell is a fishing village

THINGS TO DO

Watersports

The Centro de Buceo (diving centre) at Cala Torret runs courses in scuba diving as well as snorkelling tours by boat.
ⓐ Cala Torret ⓣ 971 18 85 28 ⓒ Dives 09.30–12.00 & 15.00–17.30 ⓘ Sites depend on weather conditions

TAKING A BREAK

Restaurants and bars

Binisafua Platja Mel £ This is a straightforward locals' bar serving excellent seafood and tapas. Worth the trip for the *llagosta amb ceba* (lobster flavoured with onion). ⓐ Centro Comercial Binisafua, Carretera Cap d'en Font, Binisafua ⓣ 971 15 18 69 ⓒ 11.00–23.00

Los Bucaneros £ This wooden bar on Binibeca beach has probably the best setting of any restaurant in Menorca – the perfect place to eat huge portions of fresh grilled fish just yards from the sea. ⓐ Platja de Binibeca ⓒ 10.00–20.00

Sa Musclera £ While away the evening in this cosy bar in the busy heart of Binibeca Vell. The atmosphere is hectic and the music loud. English beers are served along with seafood and a selection of tapas. ⓐ Binibeca Vell 33–34 ⓣ 971 18 85 55 ⓒ 12.00–02.00

Bini Grill ££ Family restaurant on the main square of the 'fishing village' serving grills, steaks and fresh fish. It gets very busy so arrive early to grab a table outside. ⓐ Binibeca Vell ⓣ 971 15 05 94 ⓒ 12.30–15.30 & 19.00–24.00

Morgana ££ Stylish restaurant with sea views and swimming pool just outside the village. Strong Menorcan flavours and lots of braised meats. ⓐ Passeig Marítim s/n ⓣ 971 15 00 61 ⓒ 13.00–23.00

Es Canutells

Following the coast road west from Binibeca there are many rocky coves and small beaches like Binisafua (see page 32), Biniparratx and Binidali, all worth a visit to escape the crowds. Es Canutells is now a quiet mixture of private villas and holiday complexes. There is a minute sandy beach situated at the mouth of a gorge, protected from the sea by high cliffs. A couple of shops sell everyday needs in the Centro Comercial.

Just inland from Binibeca and Es Canutells is the unassuming village of Sant Climent, an expat colony with English pubs, Menorcan restaurants and an excellent music bar famed throughout the island for live jazz. There is a well-stocked supermarket on the main street and high-end butchers and bakers – perfect for picking up picnic lunches. The only drawback is that the village lies directly under the flight path to the airport.

TAKING A BREAK

Restaurants & bars

Es Canutells £ Feast on seafood, salads, crêpes or omelettes on the shaded terrace of this snack bar overlooking the tiny beach. There's a children's menu and a takeaway service. ⓐ Cala Canutells ⓣ 971 18 89 34 ⓒ 09.00–00.30

Casino de Sant Climent £ Popular village restaurant and tapas bar that doubles up as a music pub with live jazz on Tuesdays attracting international musicians (from 21.30). Visitors are welcome to join in the jazz sessions. ⓐ Carrer Sant Jaume 2–4, Sant Climent ⓣ 971 15 34 18 ⓒ 06.30–late Thur–Tues

Coach and Horses £ An English village pub transported to rural Menorca. Sandwiches, snacks, hot meals and English beers are all served. You can even watch Sky Sports. Book in advance for fish and chips on Friday night. ⓐ Carrer Sant Jaume 38, Sant Climent ⓣ 971 15 33 34 ⓒ Until late

There are many rocky coves around Es Canutells

Musupta Cusi ££ Traditional restaurant run in irrepressible style in a higgledy-piggledy traditional Menorcan farmhouse with jamming sessions most days. Go for a lunch of quality tapas or savour paella on the romantic terrace by night. Carrer Musupta 80, Sant Climent 646 678 644 (mobile) 12.00–16.00 & 19.30–24.00 Booking advised

Es Molí de Foc £££ This upmarket Spanish and French restaurant has a garden that is just right for a romantic candlelit dinner. The specialities include duck breast with strawberry sauce and three types of paella. Carrer de Sant Llorenç 65, Sant Climent 971 15 32 22 www.molidefoc.com 10.00–24.00 Booking advised; closed Sun night & Mon

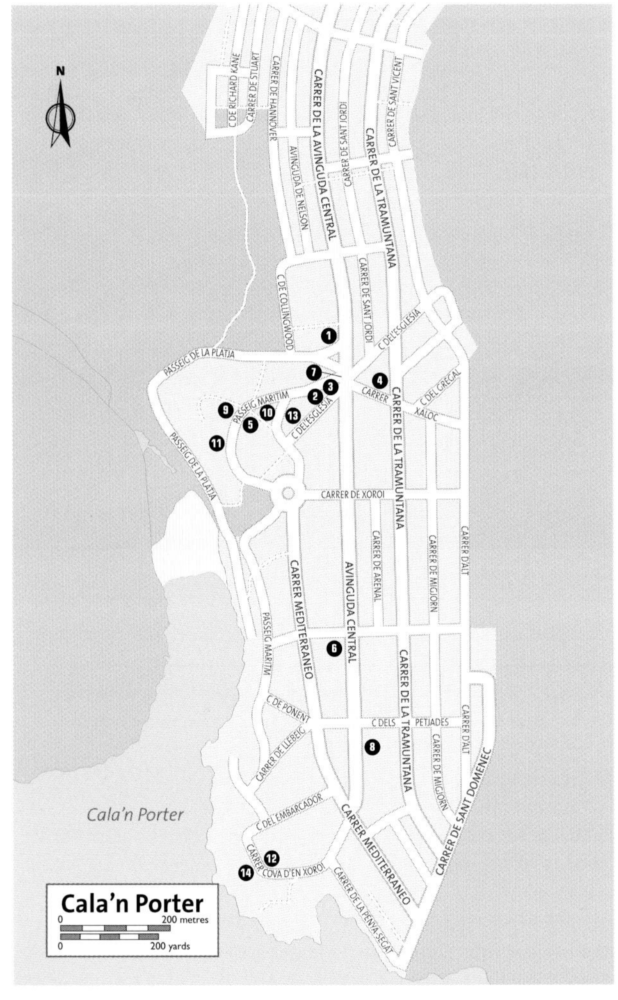
N
C DE RICHARD KANE
CARRER DE STUART
CARRER DE HANNOVER
CARRER DE LA AVINGUDA CENTRAL
CARRER DE SANT JORDI
CARRER DE LA TRAMUNTANA
CARRER DE SANT VICENT
AVINGUDA DE NELSON
C DE COLLINGWOOD
CARRER DE SANT JORDI
C DE L'ESGLESIA
PASSEIG DE LA PLATJA
PASSEIG MARITIM
C DE L'ESGLESIA
CARRER
XALOC
C DEL GREGAL
CARRER DE LA TRAMUNTANA
PASSEIG DE LA PLATJA
CARRER DE XOROI
CARRER DE ARENAL
CARRER DE MIGJORN
CARRER D'ALT
AVINGUDA CENTRAL
CARRER MEDITERRANEO
PASSEIG MARITIM
C DE PONENT
CARRER DE LLEBEIG
C DELS PETJADES
CARRER DE LA TRAMUNTANA
CARRER DE MIGJORN
CARRER D'ALT
CARRER DE SANT DOMENEC
C DEL EMBARCADOR
CARRER MEDITERRANEO
CARRER COVA D'EN XOROI
CARRER DE LA PENYA SEGAT
Cala'n Porter
Cala'n Porter
0
200 metres
0
200 yards
1
2
3
4
5
6
7
8
9
10
11
12
13
14

Cala'n Porter

A large resort by Menorcan standards and one of the oldest on the island, Cala'n Porter is situated on the south coast. The setting of Cala'n Porter is magnificent – tall, pine-studded cliffs on either side of a wide sandy beach, with a stream tumbling from a limestone gorge to run across the beach into a crystal-clear sea. The cliffs on the east side are home to restaurants, shops and bars, while those on the west are still totally undeveloped.

The best views in Cala'n Porter are from the Cova d'en Xoroi, a natural cave in the side of the cliff that acts as a bar by day and a disco by night (see page 41). This is one of the trendiest and most beautiful spots on the island, with wonderful views down the coast. Don't miss it. The cave itself is the setting for one of Menorca's most enduring folk legends. The story goes that Xoroi, a one-eared Moorish pirate, was shipwrecked at Cala'n Porter and hid inside this cave. One night he kidnapped a beautiful maiden. They lived together inside the cave for many years and she bore him three children, but one day Xoroi's footprints in the winter snow gave away his hiding place. To avoid capture, Xoroi and his son leapt into the sea, never to be seen again.

BEACHES

On the beach at Cala'n Porter you can hire sunbeds, parasols and pedaloes, and you'll find a handful of beachside restaurants and bars. From the eastern cliffs, near the Cova d'en Xoroi, a path leads to two small shingle beaches at Cales Coves where there is good snorkelling and swimming.

THINGS TO SEE

Cales Coves

This rocky cove just east of Cala'n Porter is best known for the many burial caves that were carved out of its rock in ancient times.

TAKING A BREAK

Restaurants & bars

Fun House £ ❶ Family-orientated bar complete with a soft play area for children, bouncy castle, table tennis and a pool table, just around the corner from all the other restaurants. ⓐ Avinguda Central 367 ⓣ 606 023 234 (mobile) ⓛ 11.00–15.00 & 18.00–late

Lorengo £ ❷ Friendly family restaurant serving international cuisine and good Spanish paella. ⓐ Passeig Marítim 6 ⓣ 971 37 71 96 ⓛ 10.00–16.00 & 18.30–23.30

The Patio Pub £ ❸ Friendly, Scottish-run pub serving good-value British breakfasts and beans on toast plus some Spanish dishes. The bar has satellite TV as well as English and Irish beers. ⓐ Passeig Marítim 4 ⓣ 971 37 72 06 ⓛ 19.00–early hours

Village Pub £ ❹ A typical British pub, with entertainment evenings. It stays open all day, serving everything from full English breakfasts to good-value main meals, such as shepherd's pie and toad-in-the-hole, to eat in or take away. ⓐ Carrer Xaloc 24 ⓣ 971 37 71 29 ⓛ 08.30–23.30

Bombay Star ££ ❺ All the old favourites from chicken tikka masala to kormas, pakoras and keema naan. Take your pick of rice, chips or salad to accompany your curry. ⓐ Passeig Marítim 13 ⓣ 971 37 73 46 ⓛ 18.00–late

Bar del Sur ££ ❻ À la carte restaurant that also serves tapas. ⓐ Avinguda Central 83 ⓣ 971 37 71 62 ⓛ 12.00–late

El Pulpo ££ ❼ The name of this restaurant means 'The Octopus', and the speciality is seafood served on a shady terrace beneath the palm trees. There is occasional live music. ⓐ Avinguda Central 347 ⓣ 971 37 71 10 ⓛ 12.00–16.00 & 19.00–24.00

SHOPPING

Ca N'Andreu

This shop has a good selection of souvenirs, including pottery, jewellery, carved olive wood and Menorca T-shirts. ⓐ Carrer Xaloc 3 ⓑ 10.00–13.30, 17.00–21.00

Spar

This centrally located supermarket on Avinguda Central stocks everything from Heinz baked beans and English newspapers to blow-up whales. ⓑ 08.00–21.00 Mon–Sat, 08.00–14.00 Sun

Sa Paissa ££ ❽ Popular family restaurant in the centre of the resort with an extensive menu of home-cooked food including a good choice of vegetarian dishes and a children's menu. It has a swimming pool with sunbeds, and evening entertainment. There's also simple B&B accommodation. ⓐ Avinguda Central 54 ⓣ 971 37 73 89 ⓦ www.sapaissa.com ⓑ 09.00–23.30

La Salamandra ££ ❾ Family-orientated restaurant, with swings for the children, on a large terrace on the main street. The bar attached to the restaurant has a dance floor and DJ. ⓐ Passeig Marítim s/n ⓣ 971 37 74 53 ⓑ 12.00–24.00 (bar opens 22.00)

Seagram's ££ ❿ Tired of paella and grilled sardines? Ring the changes with barbecued ribs, fajitas and deep-pan pizzas at this American-style 'eating and watering hole'. ⓐ Carrer Mediterraneo 13 ⓣ 971 37 73 59 ⓑ 12.00–24.00

La Vela ££ ⓫ Great little tapas bar with a serene dining room and a flower-filled terrace with a few tables outside. Go for the meatballs and *patatas bravas* (potatoes fried in paprika and garlic). ⓐ Passeig Marítim 5 ⓣ 971 37 74 52 ⓑ 12.00–late

Pick of the beaches – Cala'n Porter

La Palette £££ ⓬ This seafood restaurant is just outside the main hub next to the Cova d'en Xoroi (see opposite) and serves grilled prawns, peppers stuffed with fish, and salmon in champagne sauce. There's a pretty garden around the back. ⓐ Carrer Cova d'en Xoroi Y-17 ⓣ 971 37 71 37 ⓗ 12.00–23.30

AFTER DARK

Bars & clubs

Flava Bar £ ⓭ Takeaway food and noisy music nightly in the busy bar.

Thursday night is karaoke time. ⓐ Passeig Marítim 9 ⓣ 626 808 545 (mobile) ⓒ 10.00–late

Cova d'en Xoroi ££ ⓮ After nightfall this popular lookout spot (ⓒ 10.30–21.00 ⓘ Admission charge) turns into a disco, with everything from soul to rave music on a dance floor perched above the sea. Cova d'en Xoroi is the perfect spot to watch the sun go down – catch übercool DJ Ibizabla's weekly Saturday house sessions. ⓐ Carrer Cova d'en Xoroi 9 ⓣ 971 37 72 36 ⓦ www.covadenxoroi.com ⓒ Bar all day; disco 21.00–dawn ⓘ Admission charge includes one drink

Son Bou

About 3 km (2 miles) of pale golden sand between rocky headlands makes Son Bou the longest beach on Menorca. The eastern end of the beach, where the hotels and shops are found, is always busy, but as you go west the beach becomes wilder, backed by sand dunes and freshwater marshes, now a conservation area supporting a large population of migrant birds.

The resort generally needs a lick of paint but has all the facilities you need for a seaside holiday – beach bars hiring out sunbeds, shops selling buckets and spades, safe swimming, and opportunities for windsurfing and water-skiing. Behind the marshes is the Club San Jaime, an entertainment centre at the heart of a tourist village, with restaurants and bars, a waterslide for children and a disco at night (see opposite). There are a couple of quality shops on Cuesta San Jaime; buy children's clothes from Bini and leather flip-flops from Timberland.

The long golden beach of Son Bou

Visitors have been drawn to Son Bou for thousands of years; the prehistoric remains on the beach and scattered around the nearby countryside are fascinating reminders of Menorca's past.

BEACHES

Only one – but what a beach! As you head west from the seafront hotels, the beach becomes quieter and there are far fewer people wearing far fewer clothes. The western half of the beach is unofficially nudist. If you tire of Son Bou, a brisk half-hour walk from the western end leads around the headland to another fine beach at Sant Tomàs (see page 46). There is also a bus service that goes to Sant Tomàs from Centro Comercial.

THINGS TO SEE & DO

Basilica Paleocristiana (Paleo-Christian Basilica)

The remains of this 5th-century church were discovered hidden in the sand in 1951 and are enclosed by a low stone wall. Walk right around the outside, peering in at the ancient stone pillars and the enormous baptismal font carved from a single block of stone. The basilica is located at the eastern end of the beach, next to a large hotel. Look up the cliffs to see the cave houses in the hillside. Some are still occupied.

Bou Bowl

The bowling alley is a popular youngsters' hangout, with 16 bowling lanes. Expect loud Euro-pop.

ⓐ Parcela 3HC, Urbanización Son Bou (behind Cuesta San Jaime)
ⓣ 659 224 286 ⓛ 16.00–02.00 Mon–Sat, 16.00–23.00 Sun

Club San Jaime

The winding water-chute here is thrilling, and children are guaranteed to want to go on it again and again. There is also an unusual wooden labyrinth, whose interlocking patterns change weekly. Adults can eat,

swim or relax in the beautifully landscaped gardens where views stretch over the marshes down to the sea. A nightclub kicks off after dark.
ⓐ In the Club San Jaime apartment complex ⓣ 971 37 27 87
ⓛ 10.00–22.00; Waterslides 10.00–17.00; Maze 11.30–22.00

Torre d'en Galmés
This prehistoric settlement, dating from 1500 BC, is one of the biggest archaeological sites in the Balearic islands. It is reached via a footpath leading right around the site, which includes three well-preserved *talayots* (circular watchtowers), a broken *taula* (T-shaped stone monument) and an ingenious water collection system. The views are spectacular. At one time this 'village' was home to 1,000 people and may have been the capital of Menorca.
ⓐ About 5 km (3 miles) outside Son Bou from the main road to Alaior
ⓣ 902 92 90 15 ⓛ 10.00–14.30 Mon & Sun, 10.00–20.00 Tues–Sat
ⓘ Admission charge (free on Sunday)

TAKING A BREAK

Restaurants & bars
Bou Hai £ Magical Hawaiian-style cocktail bar with straw parasols where some of the waiters wear roller-skates. The drinks menu includes fresh watermelon, pear and carrot juices as well as alcoholic cocktails.
ⓐ Centro Comercial ⓣ 971 37 15 72 ⓛ 15.00–03.30

Cafeteria Club San Jaime £ This cafeteria is near the swimming pool and is a great place to eat when your children have finished in the pool and on the waterslides. ⓐ In Club San Jaime (see page 43) ⓣ 971 37 13 75
ⓛ 10.00–23.00

Las Dunas £ A good selection of international cuisine, such as prawn cocktail, spaghetti and roast lamb, at this friendly terrace restaurant close to the beach. ⓐ Centro Comercial ⓣ 971 37 16 65
ⓛ 09.00–24.00

Mai Tai Pub Cocteleria £ Hidden away on the top floor of the Centro Comercial, Mai Tai pours a good pint as well as offering fancy cocktails. There is internet access. ⓐ Centro Comercial ⓣ 971 37 23 01 ⓑ 12.00–00.30

Atalis ££ With views of the beach, this restaurant and bar is fronted by a blue-and-white awning. Go for the paella and excellent *caldereta* (lobster stew, see page 62). ⓐ Centro Comercial ⓣ 971 37 16 65 ⓑ 12.00–24.00

Boni ££ The speciality is seafood at this old-world restaurant and pizzeria with wooden seats, pretty local tiles and a great view of the sea. ⓐ Centro Comercial ⓣ 971 37 22 77 ⓑ 12.00–24.00

Son Bou ££ Salmon, steaks, sandwiches and a children's menu are served on a shady terrace in the resort's main shopping centre. ⓐ Centro Comercial ⓣ 971 37 25 03 ⓑ 10.00–24.00

Il Gondoliere £££ Smart, popular pizzeria and Italian restaurant. ⓐ Urbanización San Jaime ⓣ 971 37 20 00 ⓑ 18.00–23.00

AFTER DARK

Clubs

Copacabana ££ Disco and cocktail bar with wonderful views over the coast. ⓐ Centro Comercial ⓣ 971 37 80 47 ⓑ 17.00–03.00

Son Bou ££ This disco is lively on Thursday, Friday and Saturday nights and showcases DJs. ⓐ Centro Comercial ⓑ 23.00–04.00 ⓘ Admission charge

Club San Jaime £££ The disco inside the San Jaime apartment complex plays a wide range of music to appeal to all ages and tastes. ⓐ San Jaime apartment complex ⓑ 24.00–05.00 ⓘ Admission charge

Sant Tomàs

Sant Tomàs (Santo Tomas in Spanish) is the smallest and quietest of the main south-coast resorts, reached by a twisting drive through pine woods from the little town of Es Migjorn Gran. Everything at Sant Tomàs is centred on a single main street, with apartments, shops and restaurants on each side and the beach just a short walk away between the sand dunes.

The attraction here is the superb beach, covered in soft white sand and perfect for swimming or sunbathing. But if it looks too good to be true, it is – a freak storm in 1989 removed all of the sand and what you lie on today was imported.

Just inland, Es Migjorn Gran, with its pastel-coloured terraced houses in a maze of narrow streets, is a good place to soak up the atmosphere of

The white sandy beach and dunes at Sant Tomàs

a rural Menorcan town. The main square, Sa Plaça, is lined with bars and cafés as well as the parish church of St Christopher. This simple cream-and-white church, with its bell tower topped by a cockerel, looks much more Greek than Spanish, and the whole town has a classic Mediterranean feel.

BEACHES

The main beach at Sant Tomàs is one of the best on the island – you can hire sunbeds, parasols and pedaloes here, and there are also a couple of good bars. At the west end, beyond Bar Es Bruc, the beach becomes known as Sant Adeodato; after this, past the rocky island offshore, is Binigaus Beach, where swimming is not recommended because of the currents. From the other end of Sant Tomàs's beach you can walk to the beach at Son Bou, about 30 minutes away over the headland (see page 42).

The unspoiled beaches beyond Bar Es Bruc reach right up to the fields – but be warned: the second beach, Binigaus, is very popular with nudists.

THINGS TO DO

Pony Club

This farm offers riding lessons and pony trekking.
ⓐ Parela H9 s/n, Sant Tomàs (just off the main road) ⓣ 676 688 578
ⓛ 10.00–12.00 & 17.00–19.00 ⓘ Booking advised; closed Fri

TAKING A BREAK

Restaurants & bars

Bar Es Bruc £ Beach bar with simple food, such as sausages and burgers, and wonderful views out to sea. The place to watch the sun going down.
ⓐ On the beach ⓣ 971 37 04 88 ⓛ 10.00–16.00 (food); 10.00–23.00 (drinks)

SHOPPING

Galería d'Art

Owned by the British watercolour artist Graham Byfield, this gallery has exhibitions of his work and other local artists. ⓐ Carrer Sant Llorenç 12, Es Migjorn Gran ⓣ 971 37 03 64 ⓛ 10.00–13.00 Mon–Fri

Las Dunas £ Popular family restaurant with pool tables, crazy golf, a children's disco at 20.00 and a show at 21.00. The food is mostly pizzas and pasta dishes. ⓐ Platja Sant Tomàs ⓣ 971 37 03 70 ⓛ 12.30–15.00, 18.30–22.30

Pizzeria Il Forno £ A busy pizzeria popular with families and youngsters for early-evening chatter and crispy pizzas. A takeaway service is available. ⓐ Lord Nelson Aparthotel, Platja Sant Tomàs ⓣ 971 37 02 25 ⓛ 12.00–24.00

Ca Na Pilar ££ The locals frequent this restaurant because of its imaginative and quality Menorcan home cooking.
ⓐ Avinguda de la Mar 1, Es Migjorn Gran ⓣ 971 37 02 12 ⓛ 20.00–23.00 ⓘ Booking advised

Chic ££ This tapas bar and restaurant with a pretty garden terrace, in the heart of Es Migjorn Gran, is popular with locals and visitors alike. Choose from a wide range of traditional appetisers.
ⓐ Carrer Major 71, Es Migjorn Gran ⓣ 971 37 01 29 ⓛ 12.00–15.00 & 19.30–23.00 Tues–Sun

Lady Hamilton ££ Tucked away inside the Hamilton Court apartment complex, this cheery restaurant serves pizza, pasta and lots of yummy *bocadillos* (sandwiches). ⓐ Hamilton Court, Platja Sant Tomàs ⓣ 971 37 00 86 ⓛ 09.30–23.30

Es Pins ££ A fish restaurant overlooking the beach, with friendly service and fantastic views. Try the seafood paella. ⓐ Platja Sant Tomàs ⓣ 971 37 05 41 ⓛ 12.30–16.00 & 18.30–22.30

S'Engolidor ££ This hugely popular family-run restaurant on a garden terrace behind a small Menorcan townhouse only has a few tables, so booking is essential. The food is traditional Menorcan, the waiting staff are friendly and the views are superb. Considered one of the best restaurants on the island. ⓐ Carrer Major 3, Es Migjorn Gran ⓣ 971 37 01 93 ⓛ 19.30–22.30 Tues–Sun

Costa Sur £££ This formal restaurant overlooking the pretty pool and massive palm tree in the Santo Tomàs Hotel is the place to come for a special night out. It serves classic Spanish dishes, such as salmon and roast lamb, in an elegant dining room or on the shady terrace. ⓐ Santo Tomàs Hotel ⓣ 971 37 03 26 ⓛ 12.30–15.30 & 19.00–22.30

AFTER DARK

Bars & clubs

Admirals Pub £ This busy nightclub plays a mixture of gentle pop and rave music. In July and August it is packed out with teenagers, but at other times it is popular with people of all ages. ⓐ First floor, Hotel Victoria Platja, Platja Sant Tomàs ⓣ 971 37 02 00 ⓛ 23.00–03.00

Malibu ££ Hawaiian-style beach bar with straw roof and parasols, managed by the four-star Santo Tomàs Hotel. ⓐ Platja Sant Tomàs ⓣ 971 37 00 25 ⓛ 10.00–23.30

Victory Club ££ This smart disco, decked out with portholes and prints of Nelson, attracts all ages and plays all the latest sounds. ⓐ Lord Nelson Apparthotel, Platja Sant Tomàs ⓣ 971 37 01 25 ⓛ 22.30–03.00 Thur

Cala Galdana

Cala Galdana – also known as Santa Galdana – has been called the 'queen of Menorca's coves' and its setting is spectacular. The river Santa Galdana runs down to a small marina at the western end of the beach, a sweeping horseshoe of golden sand nestled between tall limestone cliffs with pine trees reflected in the sea. This is one of the most beautiful resort beaches on Menorca's entire coastline.

Until relatively recently there was not even a road here – but now Cala Galdana has grown into a busy resort, with villas and apartments climbing up the hillsides and enough facilities to keep everyone happy. The dramatic scenery of the bay and the south coast can be viewed from vantage points on the clifftops, while the wide beach, with its calm water and gently shelving sand, is ideal for swimming. There are several beach bars, a wide range of watersports, pedaloes for hire, mini-golf and a waterslide for the children. Cala Galdana is a good base for gentle walks to some of the quieter coves along this stretch of coastline, or inland between the walls of the Algendar Gorge (see opposite).

BEACHES

The beach at Cala Galdana has all that you could wish for, but there are several quieter beaches that can be reached on foot.

A 20-minute walk from the eastern cliffs takes you to **Cala Mitjana**, where adventurous swimmers can go right inside the limestone caves. There are no beach facilities here. Cala Mitjana can also be reached by car, but you have to pay a toll for crossing private land.

> A 45-minute walk through pine-scented woods leads to the delightful cove of Cala Macarella. There's no need to take a picnic – the Café Susy is right on the beach and rents out parasols and sunbeds. Scenic Cala Mitjana is found to the east of Santa Galdana (see above). Both coves are also accessible by road.

The footpath opposite Hotel Audax leads to **Cala Macarella**, where there is a beach bar and several caves cut into the cliffs. Just over the headland is the unspoiled cove of Cala Macarelleta, a lovely hideaway spot an hour's hot walk from Cala Galdana.

THINGS TO SEE & DO

Boat trips

Yachts make regular trips along the south coast, stopping at beautiful Cala Trebalúger for swimming, snorkelling and a picnic on the beach.
ⓐ Blue Mediterraneum ⓣ 609 305 314 ◷ Trips 10.00–13.30 & 14.00–17.30

Gorge visit

Follow the Passeig del Riu away from the beach to discover the deep limestone Barranco de Algendar (Algendar Gorge), carved out by the marshy river Santa Galdana. This spectacular gorge runs for 6 km (4 miles). Walk along the banks for wonderful views, especially at sunset. In spring and early summer the gorge buzzes with butterflies and birds and is covered with wild flowers.

Mini-train

The Cala Galdana Express mini-train is a fun way to explore – and it takes you to some spectacular viewpoints.
ⓐ Departures from behind the beach every 45 minutes ◷ 10.00–13.00 & 17.00–22.00

Viewpoints

Two lookout points above Cala Galdana both offer spectacular views. The Mirador des Riu looks down over the Algendar river and gorge, while the Mirador de Sa Punta gives sweeping views of the entire bay and right across the sea to Mallorca. Both miradors are signposted and can be reached by car or by climbing the steep steps from the beach.

Watersports

Motorboats, dinghies, windsurfing boards and snorkelling equipment can all be hired on the beach. Diving lessons are available from the Submorena diving school.

ⓐ Submorena diving school, Passeig del Riu 7 ⓣ 609 30 37 60 ⓦ www.submorenadivers.de ⓛ Dives 09.30–12.00, 15.00–17.30, May–Sept ⓘ Sites depend on weather conditions

TAKING A BREAK

Restaurants & bars

Bluecafé £ This health-food café on the sunny terrace of Hotel Rtm Audax is adjoined to the spa and wellness centre. Juices, smoothies, veggie dishes and quality salads are served all day. ⓐ Hotel Rtm Audax Spa & Wellness Centre, Urbanización Serpentona s/n ⓣ 971 15 46 46 ⓦ www.rtmhotels.com ⓛ 09.30–23.00

Chiringuito Toni £ The best of the beach bars, tucked away beneath the cliffs towards the eastern end of the beach. A romantic place to eat paella as you watch the sun set over the sea. ⓐ On the beach ⓣ 971 15 46 32 ⓛ 10.30–23.00

Tobogán £ This buzzing pizzeria beside the marina is a great place to take children as it has a waterslide, playground and mini-golf course. There is also internet access. ⓐ Platja Cala Galdana ⓣ 971 15 46 16 ⓛ 09.30–23.30

Alexandra ££ Inside the Hotel Audax, this cool restaurant offers top-quality Spanish cuisine, both buffet and à la carte. Entertainment is laid on most evenings in season. ⓐ Hotel Rtm Audax Spa & Wellness Centre, Urbanización Serpentona s/n ⓣ 971 15 46 46 ⓦ www.rtmhotels.com ⓛ 09.30–23.00

Sa Lluna ££ Halfway up the hill behind Hotel Audax, Sa Lluna's menu includes pizza, pasta and paella. There is a good-value children's menu

Cala Galdana beach has lots to offer

and a great little pool to cool off in, with tables scattered around the sunny terrace. Ⓐ Carrer Costa d'es Mirador Ⓣ 971 15 45 31 Ⓛ 11.30–late

El Mirador ££ Scenic and popular seafood restaurant perched on a rocky outcrop overlooking the beach – from the miradors on the hillside you would think this was an island. Ⓐ Over the footbridge opposite the Hotel Audax Ⓣ 971 15 45 03 Ⓛ 10.00–late (bar); 12.00–23.00 (restaurant)

AFTER DARK

Bars

Planetario ££ Smooth cocktail bar in the lobby of the Cala Galdana Hotel. A great place to kick-start an evening *paseo* around the little harbour or end the evening with a nightcap. Ⓐ Cala Galdana Ⓣ 971 15 45 00 Ⓦ www.hotelcalagaldana.com Ⓛ 10.00–23.00

Cala'n Bosch, Cala Blanca & Cala Santandría

Life at Cala'n Bosch revolves around the marina, lined with restaurants and bars where you can watch the yachts bob up and down. Next door is the quiet, upmarket mini-resort of Son Xoriguer, with a couple of smart restaurants and expensive hotels. The cliffs beside the lighthouse at Cap d'Artrutx, close to Cala'n Bosch, are a great place to watch the sun set into the sea with the mountains of Mallorca silhouetted against the sky.

Nearby Cala Blanca has suffered from excessive development but has a charming pine-fringed cove lined with terraced restaurants and bars.

Cala Santandría is little more than a handful of restaurants and bars clustered around a tiny scrap of golden sand and a rocky inlet where the people of Ciutadella come at weekends. Cala Santandría is linked to the smaller cove of Sa Caleta, whose beach is overlooked by an old watch-tower. This was the site of a French invasion of Menorca in 1756. Nowadays it is a peaceful spot with a sandy beach at the end of a long inlet, and the only invaders are people looking to soak up the sun.

BEACHES

The beach at Cala'n Bosch is wide and sandy and deepens only gradually, making it safe for swimming. A ten-minute walk, or a ride on the mini-train (which stops just behind the beach), leads you to the soft sand of Son Xoriguer where there are bars, shops and a watersports centre.

The white sand and safe, shallow water at Cala Blanca make this beach a popular choice for families. Strong swimmers can explore the sea caves in the surrounding limestone cliffs. Sa Caleta has a pocket-sized sandy beach or you can walk around the cliffs to the slightly larger beach at Cala Santandría.

THINGS TO DO

Aquarock & Kartingrock

Fun for all the family. Swimming pools, slides, jacuzzi, wave pools and games. Great karting track, single and double go-karts.
ⓐ Cala'n Bosch ⓣ 971 38 78 22 ⓦ www.aquarockmenorca.com
ⓛ 10.30–22.30 (summer); 10.30–18.00 (winter)

Boat trips

Various excursions are available from the marina at Cala'n Bosch, taking you along the south coast to swim at unspoiled beaches such as Arenal de Son Saura and Cala en Turqueta. Try Don Pancho's glass-bottomed boats for twice-daily excursions (ⓣ 619 081 445).

Diving

English-speaking and accredited PADI (Professional Association of Diving Instructors) training centre.
ⓐ Dive Cala Blanca, Cala Blanca ⓦ www.divecalablanca.com
ⓣ 617 656 906

Watersports

Sailing, windsurfing, canoeing, parasailing and water-skiing from Son Xoriguer beach, including special lessons for children.
ⓐ Surf & Sail Menorca Watersports Centre, Platja Son Xoriguer
ⓣ 971 38 70 90 ⓦ www.surfsailmenorca.com

TAKING A BREAK

Restaurants & bars

China Town £ Menorca's original Cantonese restaurant is still going strong. There is a pretty veranda covered with fairy lights for eating outside. ⓐ Es Lago, Cala'n Bosch ⓣ 971 38 57 06 ⓛ 18.00–24.00

Las Tapas £ Top-quality spicy tapas served all day, plus a choice of burgers and *bocadillos*. Grab a seat on the busy terrace to watch the boats bobbing in the marina. ⓐ Es Lago, Cala'n Bosch ⓣ 971 38 71 77 ⓛ 10.00–23.00 (May–Oct)

Café Balear ££ Popular seafood restaurant beside the marina, serving everything from grilled lobster to squid in monkfish sauce. ⓐ Cala'n Bosch ⓣ 608 744 816 ⓛ 10.00–23.30 ⓘ Closed Mon

Es Caliu ££ Large, rustic restaurant on the main road to Ciutadella; the speciality is charcoal grills and it's full of Menorcan families on Sunday lunchtimes. ⓐ Carretera Cala Blanca, near the turn-off for Cala Blanca ⓣ 971 38 01 65 ⓛ 13.00–16.00 & 19.00–23.30

Ca'n Anglada ££ Friendly restaurant with a wide range of Menorcan specialities – try the special paella. ⓐ Es Lago, Cala'n Bosch ⓣ 971 38 14 02 ⓛ 12.00–13.30 & 18.00–24.00

Complejo Es Mirador ££ Local cuisine overlooking the pretty beach and cove at Cala Blanca, with barbecues every evening at the tropical-themed Bar Key West and a swimming pool for the children. ⓐ Platja de Cala Blanca ⓣ 971 38 62 62 ⓛ 09.00–03.00

Cova Sa Nacra ££ This cool, shady cliff-side bar and restaurant overlooks Cala Santandría. The restaurant serves tasty fish and meat dishes. ⓐ Cala Santandría ⓣ 971 38 62 06 ⓛ 10.30–24.00

Sa Quadra ££ Top-quality Menorcan cuisine at reasonable prices. Vegetarian and children's menus, and shady terrace. ⓐ Cala Santandría beach ⓣ 971 48 09 59 ⓛ 12.00–24.00

Es Test de na Silvie ££ A special treat; eat outdoors under an awning or inside in a smart, creamy-coloured dining room. Enjoy fresh prawns, tender steak and delicious pastas. ⓐ Avinguda Portixol 21–22, Es Lago,

Cala'n Bosch 971 38 78 95 13.00–16.00 & 19.00–23.00
Closed Wed

Aquarium £££ A sophisticated seafood restaurant on the right-hand side of the marina, taking its name from the massive fish tanks at the back of the dining room. Choose from bowls of steaming mussels or lobster stew, and accompany with a fine dry white wine. Es Lago, Cala'n Bosch 971 38 74 42 10.30–23.00

AFTER DARK

Bars & clubs

Bar Key West £ Tropical-themed bar serving sticky cocktails with a great view over the sandy cove at Cala Blanca. Platja de Cala Blanca 971 38 62 62 18.00–03.00

Big Apple ££ Early evening is great for family karaoke; later a disco bar perfect for late teens. Carrer de Tramuntana, Cala'n Bosch 17.00–04.00; disco starts at 24.00

Moonlight ££ Live music on the terrace and colourful cocktails. Avinguda Cala Blanca, Cala Blanca 10.00–03.00

The Marina – focal point of Cala'n Bosch

Cala'n Bruch & Cala'n Forcat

The rugged coastline to the northwest of Ciutadella is studded with rocky coves and fjord-like inlets of crystal-clear water. This area has grown rapidly in recent years to become one of Menorca's liveliest holiday centres, with a wide choice of restaurants, bars and nightlife. However, just inland, you can still see the fields dotted with dry-stone sheep shelters shaped like pyramids.

There are four separate coves here – the Blue Flag beach at Cala'n Blanes, complete with reggae bar, Cala'n Bruch (also known as Cala En Brut), Cala'n Forcat and tiny Cales Piques. Over the years, the four have merged into one mega-resort, centred on the Los Delfines complex.

A fjord-like inlet at Cala'n Bruch

Plaça d'Espanya, at the heart of Los Delfines, has shops, restaurants and even an open-air chapel. From here, it is a short walk to any of the four beaches – and if you don't fancy the walk, you can always hop on the mini-train that tours the streets at regular intervals. These resorts make a great base for a fun-filled family holiday, with everything you need to keep people of all ages amused – and the elegant city of Ciutadella is just a short bus ride away.

BEACHES

Each of the four coves has its own tiny beach. The beach at Cala'n Blanes is small and sandy, with sunbeds, parasols and pedaloes for hire and shady pine woods bordering the sand. Cala'n Bruch has very little sand, but platforms above the long, narrow creek are perfect for sunbathing, and the lower platforms are good for diving into the clear water. Cala'n Forcat has a wide, sandy beach at the edge of a tiny cove, while Cales Piques has a small beach reached by a flight of narrow steps.

THINGS TO DO

Get sporty

Hire mountain bikes and canoes by the hour or learn to dive just off the shallow beach. There are also guided walking tours along the coastline.
ⓐ Club Hotel Almirante Farragut, Cala'n Forcat ⓣ 971 38 80 00
🕒 09.00–21.00

Los Delfines Aquapark

Swimming pools with slides, crazy golf, open-air jacuzzis, playgrounds, mini-karting, bars, a restaurant and endless other attractions for all the family.
ⓐ Urbanización los Delfines, Cala'n Blanes ⓣ 971 38 82 51 (Aquapark); 971 38 87 05 (restaurant) ⓦ www.aquacenter-menorca.com
🕒 10.30–18.30

TAKING A BREAK

Restaurants & bars

Ca'n Moll £ Menorcan fish dishes, such as grilled hake, rabbit in almond sauce and chicken with prawns, as well as a wide range of pizzas served on a garden terrace. Just out of the bustle of Los Delfines; there is also a children's play terrace. ⓐ Avinguda Simón de Olivar 97, Cala'n Blanes ⓣ 971 38 84 90 Ⓛ 17.00–23.00

Churchill's £ A good old British pub where you can sit back and relax. A selection of decent pub grub is available. Bouncy castle, pool tables and games room. ⓐ Avinguda Cales Piques 225, Cala'n Blanes ⓣ 971 38 87 54 ⓦ www.churchillsbar.co.uk Ⓛ 13.00–01.30

Indiana Bill £ A fast-food restaurant, with an adjoining children's play area. ⓐ Carrer d'Escorel, Cala'n Blanes ⓣ 609 763 026 Ⓛ 10.00–24.00

Mannah Mannah £ A cool new juice and cocktail bar with a stylish interior. ⓐ Avinguda los Delfines, Cala'n Blanes ⓣ 680 280 526 Ⓛ 12.00–23.00

L'Ancora ££ This popular restaurant serves barbecued pizza and pasta on a shady garden terrace. Create your own breakfast in the morning to build up your strength for a day on the beach. ⓐ Avinguda Simón de Olivar, Cala'n Blanes ⓣ 971 38 84 05 Ⓛ 09.00–24.00

Grill Las Brasas ££ One of the few typically Menorcan restaurants in the area has been going for more than 20 years. Hams hang from the ceiling; wooden panels and threshers hang from the walls. Choose from pork loin or kebabs cooked over an open fire and see the place fill up with happy families as the night goes on. ⓐ Avinguda los Delfines s/n ⓣ 971 38 80 16 ⓦ www.grilllasbrasas.com Ⓛ 18.30–24.00

El Patio ££ Seafood restaurant specialising in fish (especially lobster casserole), with marvellous views out to sea. ⓐ Avinguda los Delfines s/n ⓣ 919 18 48 64 ◷ 12.00–15.30 & 18.30–23.00

Sa Caldereta ££ Menorcan classics, such as lobster stew and roast shoulder of lamb, in a family-friendly restaurant. ⓐ Avinguda los Delfines 2–11 ⓣ 971 38 82 12 ◷ 11.00–24.00

AFTER DARK

Bars & cafés

Blue Breeze £ Friendly, modern cocktail bar with pool tables and a happy hour. ⓐ Centro comercial, Avinguda Cales Piques ⓣ 971 38 81 53 ⓦ www.menorcabluebreeze.com ◷ 11.00–04.00 ⓘ Happy hour 23.00–24.00

Cheers £ This lively bar has karaoke until 24.00 followed by disco music until 04.00. ⓐ Centro comercial, Avinguda Cales Piques ⓣ 971 58 60 79 ◷ 21.00–04.00 ⓘ Happy hour 23.00–24.00

Green Parrot £ Lots of fun and frolics at this English-run bar. ⓐ Carrer des Canal, Cala'n Bruch ◷ 19.00–04.00 (disco from 24.00) ⓘ Happy hour 21.00–22.00

Sa Torreta £ A cute little late-night cocktail bar and café in a tiny whitewashed tower just off Los Delfines. Keep going late into the night with tasty crêpes and *bocadillos*. ⓐ Avinguda los Delfines 19 ⓣ 971 38 91 79 ◷ 10.00–23.00

Fornells

With its low, whitewashed cottages, fishing boats bobbing in the breeze and stately palm trees guarding a seafront promenade, Fornells is everyone's idea of a Mediterranean fishing village. The fishermen still set out from here each morning to catch the spiny lobsters that are at the heart of Menorca's most famous dish – *caldereta de langosta*, or lobster casserole (see opposite). In summer, the restaurants crowding along the promenade are full of happy eaters most afternoons and late into the night.

The villas here are built in the local style and many have attractive gardens bursting with different varieties of cactus. Between here and the village is the watersports centre of Ses Salines.

Most visitors head straight for the village itself. Built on the west side of the Bay of Fornells, with its calm waters and long natural harbour, Fornells was originally founded to defend the north coast against pirate ships. Follow the waterfront beyond the fish restaurants around the main square and you come to the ruins of a 17th-century fortress, Castell Sant Antoni. Keep going and you soon reach the headland, buffeted by wind and waves, where a tiny chapel is built into the rock and you can walk right inside a restored watchtower and imagine yourself on sentry duty looking out for enemy ships.

Many people come to Fornells to try the celebrated *caldereta*. The ingredients are simple: a lobster, tomatoes and onions, garlic and parsley. Everything is cooked in an earthenware bowl and served with wafers of dry bread to dip into the soup, and a set of tools for prising the lobster apart. Most of the restaurants in Fornells serve *caldereta* – yet each one is different and each chef guards their own recipe jealously. It is expensive, but an experience to remember – King Juan Carlos of Spain regularly sails his yacht over from his Mallorcan holiday home to eat *caldereta de langosta* at his favourite restaurant, Es Pla (see page 65). If you don't want to spend a fortune, you could try *caldereta de mariscos* – this seafood and fish casserole is cooked in the same way but without the lobster.

BEACHES

Platja de Fornells has its own small beach, 3 km (2 miles) out of town, with a footpath leading around the bay to the larger beach at Cala Tirant where a beach bar rents out sunbeds, parasols and pedaloes.

THINGS TO DO

Scuba diving

Scuba-diving courses are offered at the Diving Centre, Fornells.
ⓐ Diving Centre, Passeig Marítim 68 ⓣ 971 37 64 31
ⓦ www.divingfornells.com ⓗ Dives 09.30–12.00, 15.00–17.30
ⓘ Sites depend on weather conditions

Watersports

The Bay of Fornells is ideal for novice sailors and windsurfers because of its calm waters and gentle breezes. **Windsurf Fornells** has dinghies, catamarans and windsurfing equipment for hire and can offer lessons for beginners and more advanced sailors.
ⓐ At the entrance to the village ⓣ 971 37 64 00
ⓦ www.windsurf-fornells.de ⓗ Daily in season

Hire speedboats for a trip around the bay from **Servinautic Menorca** in Fornells marina.
ⓐ Fornells Marina ⓣ 629 27 32 09
ⓦ www.servinauticmenorca.com ⓗ Daily in season

EXCURSIONS

Cap de Cavallería

From Fornells you can follow a narrow road to Menorca's northernmost point, the lighthouse at Cap de Cavallería, where wild goats graze on rocky headlands lashed by wind and waves. Along the way you pass the old Roman port of Sanitja, now a pretty harbour, with tracks leading to the unspoiled beaches of Cavallería and Farragut.

North-coast beaches

Fornells is a good starting point for excursions to some of the wilder north-coast beaches, especially Binimel-Là and its neighbour Cala Pregonda, which can only be reached on foot or by boat.

TAKING A BREAK

Restaurants & bars

La Palma £ This bar on the main square is always packed with local families, especially for a leisurely lunch over the weekend. Fishy tapas is a good option during the week. ⓐ Plaza S'Algaret 3 ⓣ 971 37 66 34 ⓛ 07.00–24.00

S'Algaret £ Next door to La Palma in the main square, this crowded restaurant's menu offers *raciones* (main-course portions of tapas), the freshest of fish, and yes, lobster stew. ⓐ Plaza S'Algaret 7 ⓣ 971 37 66 66 ⓛ 11.00–24.00

The attractive resort of Platja de Fornells in the bay of Cala Tirant

Es Cranc ££ Where the locals choose to eat *caldereta de langosta* – no outdoor chairs and no sea views, just tremendous home cooking and a very Menorcan atmosphere. ⓐ Carrer Escoles 31 ⓣ 971 37 64 42 ◷ 13.30–16.00, 20.00–24.00

Cranc Pelut ££ Quiet, out-of-the-way restaurant serving Mediterranean dishes, such as paella, pork loin and fried squid, overlooking the bay at the end of the seafront promenade. ⓐ Passeig Marítim 98 ⓣ 971 37 67 43 ◷ 12.30–16.30, 20.00–24.00, closed Tues

Es Port ££ Lobster casserole and grilled meat and fish are the specialities at this friendly waterfront restaurant. ⓐ Avinguda Poeta Gumersindo Riera 5 ⓣ 971 37 64 03 ◷ 12.00–15.30, 19.00–23.30

S'Ancora ££ Popular fish restaurant facing the harbour. One of the set menus features a small tasting of *caldereta de langosta* at a reasonable price. ⓐ Avinguda Poeta Gumersindo Riera 7 ⓣ 971 37 66 70 ◷ 12.00–16.00, 18.00–23.00

Sa Llagosta ££ White linen tablecloths and a pristine dining room plus perfect helpings of *caldereta*. ⓐ Carrer Gabriel Gelabert 12 ⓣ 971 37 65 66 ◷ 12.00–15.30, 19.00–23.30

El Pescador £££ Fornells' most popular restaurant has wicker chairs overlooking the waterfront, a manic atmosphere and a wide variety of fish and seafood dishes as well as the ubiquitous *caldereta*. Diners are presented with paper bibs to prevent splashback! ⓐ Carrer de S'Algaret 3 ⓣ 971 37 65 38 ◷ 12.00–24.00

Es Pla £££ Imagine you're a king as you eat lobster right on the water's edge. This restaurant is formal by Menorcan standards and maintains immaculate service and produces exquisite *caldereta*.
ⓐ Passeig Marítim de Gumersind Riera ⓣ 971 37 66 55 ◷ 12.30–15.00, 20.00–22.30

Arenal d'en Castell & Son Parc

The northeast coast between Fornells and Maó is the setting for two of Menorca's biggest beaches, as well as a string of smaller bays and coves. The coastline here is backed by sand dunes, with acres of thick pine forest inland. The two large resorts have plenty of restaurants and nightlife, but much of this area is quiet and unspoiled.

Nearby Addaia is a peaceful resort set around a yacht marina at the entrance to a long, sheltered creek, and it is very laid-back in style. From Arenal d'en Castell you can walk along the coast to Son Parc, a very English beach resort boasting Menorca's only golf course and another long sandy beach. Sa Roca, a few kilometres inland, consists of a few villas in the middle of peaceful pine woods, in the shadow of Menorca's highest mountain, Monte Toro (see page 77).

BEACHES

The beaches at **Arenal d'en Castell** and **Son Parc** have some facilities and are suitable for families. A 20-minute walk from Son Parc is the pretty cove of **Cala Pudent**, where the beach is usually very quiet. Although there is no beach at Addaia, the nearby village of Na Macaret has a small square of sand and several good restaurants.

THINGS TO DO

Golf

Visitors are welcome to use Golf Son Parc, an 18-hole course, along with the driving range, putting green and tennis courts, which are floodlit at night. Club hire is available, but don't turn up to play a round in beach gear! Hire a buggy to go around the course to offset the midsummer sun.
ⓐ Golf Son Parc, on the road into Son Parc from the Me-7 road between Maó and Fornells ⓣ 971 18 88 75 ⓦ www.golfsonparc.com ⓛ 09.00–dusk (winter); 09.00–17.30 (spring & autumn); 07.00–18.00 (summer)
ⓘ By reservation only

The oyster-shaped bay of Arenal d'en Castell

S'Hort de Llucaitx Park

Hire horses and ponies to trek the riding trails deep into the countryside; try mountain biking or mini golf; let the children run riot in the little play park or they can pet the animals on the working farm.
Ⓐ Carretera Maó–Fornells km 17 Ⓣ 629 391 894 Ⓒ 10.00–19.00
Ⓘ Restaurant open weekends only

Watersports

Both Son Parc and Arenal d'en Castell have facilities for windsurfing, and sailing dinghies can be hired from the marina in Addaia.
Ulmo Diving Centre Ⓐ Port Addaia Ⓣ 971 35 90 05 Ⓒ 09.00–18.00

TAKING A BREAK

Restaurants

Pekin £ The Son Parc branch of Menorca's best Chinese restaurant. All the favourite dishes, including sweet and sour chicken, beef with oyster sauce and Peking Duck. Ⓐ Zona Comercial A2, Son Parc Ⓣ 971 36 38 49 Ⓒ 12.00–24.00 (summer)

Rex's Pub £ Homesick Brits gather at this typical English pub for hearty cooked breakfasts and snacks as well as well-poured pints. Ⓐ Zona Comercial, Son Parc Ⓣ 971 35 91 05 Ⓒ 09.00–17.00

Alcalde ££ Classic Menorcan dishes, such as roast kid and fish stew, in this restaurant overlooking the beach. ⓐ Carrer Romani s/n, Arenal d'en Castell ⓣ 971 35 80 93 ◷ 11.15–15.45 & 18.30–24.00

Restaurante Addaia ££ Flambés are the house special at this popular Spanish restaurant up the hill from the marina, with views out to sea. ⓐ Zona Comercial, Addaia ⓣ 971 35 92 61 ◷ 18.00–23.00

S'Arenal ££ Restaurant and pizzeria perched above the beach at Arenal d'en Castell, with live music every night. ⓐ Urbanización Arenal d'en Castell ⓣ 971 63 65 92 ◷ 09.00–23.00

Halalissy £££ A popular restaurant in the clubhouse at Golf Son Parc serving fresh seafood, steaks and good homemade soda breads. ⓐ Golf Son Parc, on the road into Son Parc from the Me-7 between Maó and Fornells ⓣ 971 35 93 26 ◷ 09.00–24.00; 09.00–dusk (winter) ⓘ Closed Mon

Puig de Sa Roca £££ This restaurant has a swimming pool and is hidden in pine woods. Traditional Spanish cuisine is served on a pretty and shaded veranda. There is a large indoor restaurant for dinner and a few chalet-style rooms off the courtyard. ⓐ Urbanización Sa Roca, Carretera Maó-Fornells ⓣ 971 18 86 42 ◷ 12.00–16.00 & 20.00–24.00 ⓘ Booking advisable

AFTER DARK

Bars

The Corner Bar £ This Irish pub has regular live entertainment and a large selection of Irish whiskeys. ⓐ Zona Comercial, Son Parc ⓣ 971 35 90 70 ◷ 13.00–03.00 (karaoke Sun 21.00–01.00)

Catedral de Santa Maria, Ciutadella

EXCURSIONS
Out & about

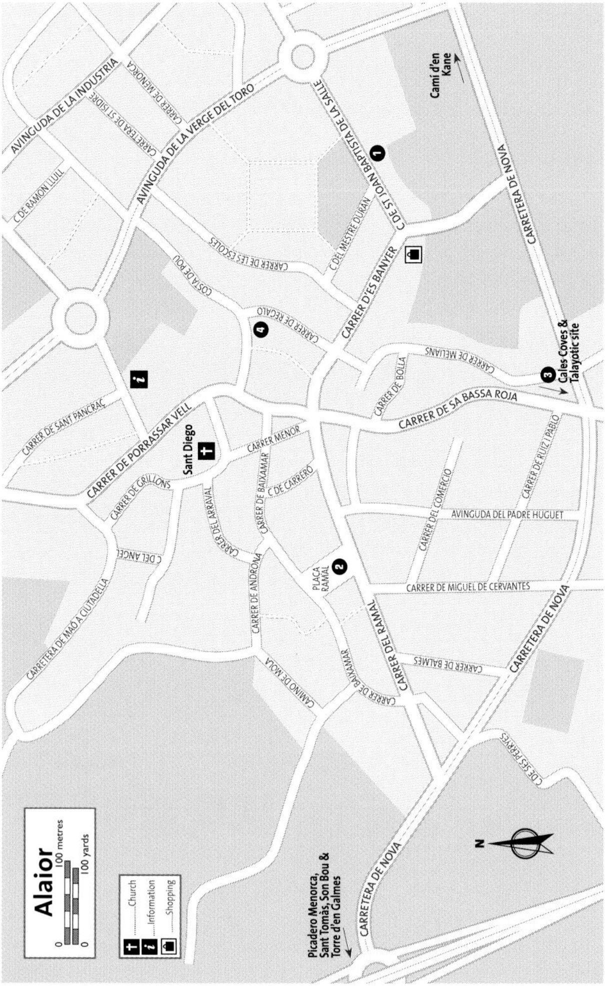

Alaior

0 100 metres
0 100 yards

Church
Information
Shopping

AVINGUDA DE LA INDUSTRIA
AVINGUDA DE LA VERGE DEL TORO
CARRER DE MENORCA
CARRETERA DE ST ISIDRE
C DE RAMON LLULL
CARRER DE LES ESCOLES
C DEL MESTRE DURAN
C DE ST JOAN BAPTISTA DE LA SALLE
CARRER D'ES BANYER
COSTA DE POU
CARRER DE REGALO
CARRER DE MELIANS
CARRER DE BOLLA
CARRER DE SA BASSA ROJA
CARRER DE RUIZ I PABLO
CARRER DE SANT PANCRAÇ
CARRER DE PORRASSAR VELL
Sant Diego
CARRER MENOR
CARRER DE GRILLONS
C DE CARRERO
CARRER DE BAIXAMAR
CARRER DEL ARRAVAL
C DEL ANGEL
CARRETERA DE MAÓ A CIUTADELLA
CARRER DEL COMERCIO
AVINGUDA DEL PADRE HUGUET
PLAÇA RAMAL
CARRER DE ANDRONA
CARRER DE MIGUEL DE CERVANTES
CARRER DEL RAMAL
CAMINO DE MOLA
CARRER DE BALMES
CARRETERA DE NOVA
C DE SES PERXES
Camí d'en Kane
Cales Coves & Talayotic site
Picadero Menorca, Sant Tomàs, Son Bou & Torre d'en Galmes
N
1
2
3
4

Alaior

Alaior (pronounced 'Allay-or') is sometimes referred to as Menorca's third capital due to its historical role as a mediator between Maó and Ciutadella, and because of the wealth and independence afforded it by its thriving leather and cheese industries.

Tourism has largely ignored the town, and few visitors actually take the time to stop and explore the cool, shaded streets of Alaior, which is on a hill just off the main road from Maó to Ciutadella. Those who do are richly rewarded by the striking architecture of its fine townhouses, the ornate Town Hall and the vast, newly renovated church of Santa Eulàlia. Be sure to see the night-time handicraft markets, the splendid views of the surrounding countryside from the water-tower and the striking church of Sant Diego, whose ancient cloisters have been converted into modern flats and whose courtyard, known as Sa Lluna, is a popular setting for the commune's concerts and folk dancing.

Alaior's main claim to fame is that it is the home of Admiral Nelson's favourite cheese, the island's renowned Mahón cheese originally named

SHOPPING

There is a **night market** in Alaior where local ceramics, leather, cotton and silver crafts are sold from stalls under strings of coloured lights, with some live demonstrations and workshops (Plaça Ramal 19.00–23.00 Wed, June–Sept).

For cheese, try the factory shop of **La Payesa** down an unlikely-looking steep backstreet (Carrer d'es Banyer 64 09.00–13.00, 16.00–19.00 Mon–Fri Closed Sat) or **Coinga** (Carrer d'es Mercadal 09.00–13.00, 16.30–20.30 Mon–Fri, 09.00–13.30 Sat).

The main shopping street, sloping little **Carrer del Ramal**, has a selection of tempting stores including **Calzados Alaior** (No 19) for trainers and leather belts, and **Blanc i Verd** (No 16) with its fine Mallorcan pearls, pottery, wood and glassware.

Quiet backstreet in Alaior

after the port (Maó, also called Mahón) where it was first made and exported. Today, the cheese is still made in the traditional way in Alaior, from recipes passed down from generation to generation. You can buy it in various stages of maturity from *fresco* (fresh and soft) to *anejo* (matured for two years, and as strong as Parmesan). The more mature types travel well and make good presents.

BEACHES

The largest beach on the island is an 8-km (5-mile) drive away at Son Bou (see page 42), and Sant Tomàs is close by (see page 46). Both beaches have all the facilities you will need for a lazy day in the sun.

THINGS TO SEE & DO

Camí d'en Kane

Menorca's first British governor, Sir Richard Kane, built a road across the island from Maó to Ciutadella – paid for by a tax on alcohol.

The first section of the road (Maó to Alaior) has been repaired, and a drive along 'Kane's road' is a good way of experiencing the typical Menorcan countryside of cattle, flower-filled meadows and undulating hillsides. From the town centre, follow Carretera de Nova eastwards and turn left off the main road from Alaior to Maó (Me-7), following signs for the 'Camí d'en Kane'. There are many walks to be taken along the route; for further details contact the tourist office.

Picadero Menorca

This popular ranch-style riding stable on the outskirts of Alaior offers pony treks, rides in a horse and cart, and lessons for children and complete beginners.

Carretera Alaior–Son Bou, just off the roundabout beneath the Me-1
608 323 566 15.00–20.00

Prehistoric treasures

The prehistoric remains near Alaior are worth exploring, particularly the secluded **Cales Coves** (see page 37), where an extraordinary honeycomb of ancient burial caves is worn out of the cliff face. From time to time, backpackers take up residence in the caves. Combine exploring the cove (you have to walk there or sail) with a long lunch at Opera Due restaurant (see below) or a trek along the coast to the Cova d'en Xoroi in Cala'n Porter (see page 41). Open access

The **Talayotic site** at Torralba d'en Salort boasts the island's most magnificent T-shaped stone structure, called a *taula*.
Carretera Alaior–Cala'n Porter 10.00–20.00, closed first Sun of month Admission charge

TAKING A BREAK

Restaurants & bars

Ca'n Jaumot £ ❶ A popular local bar, pizza and *caldereta de langosta* (lobster stew) restaurant with a great terrace for sunny evenings. Locals and expats mingle happily. Sant Joan Baptista de la Salle 6
971 37 82 94 www.restcanjaumot.restaurantesok.com
06.30–24.00

Transparent £ ❷ This trendy café-bar in a pretty, spacious square is popular with locals for tapas on weekend lunchtimes and late-afternoon coffees. There's a playground next to it to keep children amused.
Plaça Ramal 22 971 37 27 96 11.00–02.00

Opera Due Restaurante e Pizzeria ££ ❸ A welcoming ochre-coloured interior with a massive fireplace and typical Italian home cooking and pizzas. There is a lovely terrace with a swimming pool and play area for the children. Urbanización Cales Coves, Carretera Sant Climent
971 37 73 75 www.restaurante-opera.com 13.00–15.30 & 20.00–23.00 (May–Oct)

The beach at Son Bou is the largest on Menorca

The Cobblers Garden Restaurant £££ ❹ One of the best restaurants on the island, hidden in an elegant townhouse that was once the home of a famous local shoemaker. Weather permitting, traditional Menorcan menus are served in the delightful courtyard. Ⓐ Costa d'en Macari Ⓣ 971 37 14 00 Ⓛ 19.00–late Mon–Sat, Apr–Sept; closed Oct–Mar ❗ Advance booking recommended

Es Mercadal

The picturesque old market town of Es Mercadal (pronounced Es Merk-a-dal), at the geographical heart of the island, is known for its traditional crafts, classy gastronomy and the flamboyant displays of horsemanship during its dazzling July fiesta (see page 108).

The name 'Mercadal' originates from the fact that the town was once the major market town of the island where locals came to sell their fruit, vegetables and traditional wares, and to this day there remains a handicraft market held on Tuesday and Saturday afternoons. Besides farming, the main industries here are the production of *abarcas* (traditional sandals), confectionery and almond macaroons.

BEACHES

Two of Menorca's finest beaches lie within easy reach of Es Mercadal on the north coast – Binimel-là with its striking red sand and pebbles, backed by sand dunes, and Cala Pregonda, with its sandy beach and crystal-clear waters, a brisk 30-minute walk along the coast from Binimel-là (don't do it in the height of summer!).

SHOPPING

Centre Artesanal de Menorca

Quality crafts – photo frames, lamps, modern interpretations of traditional pottery designs and funky ceramics. ⓐ Recinte Firal des Mercadal ⓣ 971 15 44 36 ⓛ 09.00–14.00 Mon–Fri, 11.00–14.30 Sat (Nov–Apr); 10.00–14.00 & 17.00–20.00 Mon–Fri, 10.00–13.30 Sat (May–Oct)

Galeria del Sol

Contemporary gallery with an increasing reputation for exhibiting paintings by international and Menorcan artists. ⓐ Carrer d'es Sol ⓣ 971 37 51 25 ⓛ 10.00–14.00 & 19.00–22.00 Mon–Sat ⓘ Closed Sun

THINGS TO SEE & DO

Monte Toro

Es Mercadal is the starting point for the ascent of Monte Toro, Menorca's highest hill named after a *toro* (wild bull) that apparently led a party of nuns to a hidden cave containing a statue of the Madonna and Child. The convent at the summit is a place of pilgrimage. There is also a gift shop and café as well as a massive statue of Jesus. The views from the terrace are sensational, especially at sunset. Most days you can see the entire island and, if the visibility is especially good, Mallorca.

Old Town

As well as shopping on Carrer Nou (the main street) and lapping up the local colour on Plaça Constitució (the busy main square), be sure to explore the sleepy historic part of town where whitewashed cottages straddle an ancient reservoir built on the orders of the first British governor, Sir Richard Kane (see page 73).

Sa Farinera de s'Arangi

The museum of an old flour mill, on the main road just outside Es Mercadal, with a commercial area, a children's playground and a restaurant.
ⓐ Carretera Maó–Ciutadella ⓣ 971 15 43 08 ⓦ www.safarinera.com
ⓛ 10.00–21.00 (shops); 11.00–01.00 (playground & restaurant)

TAKING A BREAK

Restaurants, bars & bakeries

Bar Es Gurugú £ A trendy bar with blue-tinted windows and little red-topped stools, currently serving the best *pomada* (see page 97) in town! ⓐ Carrer Nou 65 ⓣ 971 37 55 87 ⓛ 18.00–23.00

Ca's Sucrer £ An old-fashioned sweet shop with jars neatly arranged on shelves around the store. There are a couple of tables outside to enjoy hot chocolate and pastries. ⓐ Plaça Constitucío 11 ⓣ 971 37 51 75 ⓛ 09.30–13.30 & 17.00–20.30 ⓘ Closed Mon

Patisseria Ca'n Pons £ This small, rather smart-looking bakery sells some of the best almond macaroons on the island. ⓐ Carrer Nou 13 ⓣ 971 37 51 75 ⓛ 09.30–13.30 & 17.00–20.30

Sa Plaça de C'an Bep £ A no-frills locals' bar in the main square, popular for morning coffee and tapas snacks at lunch. ⓐ Plaça Constitucío 2 ⓣ 971 37 50 48 ⓛ 07.00–23.30

Ets Arcs ££ Don't be put off by the exterior, there is a peaceful terrace at the back where you can enjoy generous portions of rabbit with garlic and other local dishes. ⓐ Carretera Maó–Ciutadella ⓣ 971 37 55 38 ⓛ 13.00–16.00 & 19.00–23.00

Jeni ££ A lovely yellow-painted eatery serving traditional cuisine with a modern twist; savour the rich *oli-aigüa* (garlicky tomato and bread soup) and *caldereta* (lobster stew, see page 62). There is a great pool with a jacuzzi, plus rooms and suites as well. ⓐ Carrer Mirada del Toro 81 ⓣ 971 37 50 59 ⓦ www.hostaljeni.com ⓛ 07.00–00.30

Es Molí d'es Racó ££ An atmospheric restaurant in a whitewashed windmill (which you can see from the main road), serving Menorcan specialities to locals who pack the tables at the weekend. The walls are lined with good wines and the dining tables covered with cheery blue-and-white cloths. ⓐ Carrer Major 53 ⓣ 971 37 53 92 ⓦ www.molidesraco.de ⓛ 13.00–16.00 & 19.00–23.00

Ca'n Aguedet £££ Menorcan cuisine served in a dining room gleaming with spotless napery and glassware. The wines are made on the island especially for the restaurant and you won't find them anywhere else. ⓐ Carrer Lepanto 23 ⓣ 971 37 53 91 ⓛ 13.00–16.00, 19.30–23.30

Es Mercadal was once a market town

Horses play a significant part in Menorcan tradition

Ferreries

Bustling Ferreries (pronounced 'Ferrer-ree-es') was once dependent entirely on agriculture and dairy farming. Nowadays, it has expanded and enjoys a thriving industry of shoe making, jewellery and furniture, and is a popular shopping stop en route from Maó to Ciutadella (see page 87).

The name of the town (from *ferreria*, the Catalan word for 'blacksmith') derives from its early reputation for making iron door hinges. The highest town on the island, Ferreries is also at the heart of Menorca's most fertile zone, and every Saturday morning there is a small market in Plaça Espanya where farmers from the surrounding area offer their produce of fruits, vegetables, cheeses, biscuits, honey, herbs and handicrafts. The main square – Plaça de l'Església – is one of the prettiest corners of town, flanked by the small whitewashed church of San Bartomeu and the town hall with its brightly coloured flags. The narrow jumble of sun-baked backstreets with their neatly shuttered houses has an air of typical Mediterranean tranquillity.

BEACHES

From Ferreries, by car, you can easily reach the beaches of Sant Tomàs (see page 46), neighbouring Binigaus beach (see page 47), Cala Galdana (see page 50) and nearby Cala Mitjana (see page 50).

THINGS TO SEE & DO

Binisues

The beautiful soft-yellow museum house at Binisues provides a fascinating insight into aristocratic life in bygone days. You can explore the well-tended formal gardens, and there is a first-class restaurant (see page 84) with magnificent views of central Menorca.

Camí dels Alocs, Carretera Maó–Ciutadella, Km 31.6 971 37 37 28

11.00–19.00 Admission charge; closed Mon

Centre de la Natura de Menorca (Natural History Museum)

A fascinating interactive museum with changing exhibitions on Menorca's flora and fauna, run by the Grup Balear d'Ornitologia, Menorca's environmental agency.

ⓐ Carrer Mallorca 2 ⓣ 971 37 45 05 ⓦ www.gobmenorca.com/english
🕒 10.30–13.00 & 17.30–20.30 Tues–Sat, 10.00–14.00 Sun (late May–Oct). Hours vary in winter – check with the museum. ❗ Admission charge

Espectacle Eqüestre de Menorca (Horse shows)

Marvel at the equestrian skills of the riding stables at their twice-weekly demonstrations of dressage skills, including those seen at fiestas (see page 107). There are also shows at San Martorellet, 1 km (⅔ mile) further along the same road towards Cala Galdana (🕒 20.30 Tues & Thur).

ⓐ Carretera Cala Galdana, Km 0.5 ⓣ 971 15 50 59
ⓦ www.showmenorca.com 🕒 Shows 20.30 Wed & Sun (June–Sept)
❗ Admission charge

Go-karting

Children of all ages love whizzing around the go-kart tracks at Costa Nova Go Karting Club. Two-person karts for parents with small children and karts for people with disabilities are available.

ⓐ Costa Nova Go Karting Club, Carretera Maó–Ciutadella, Km 35
ⓣ 971 38 04 24 🕒 10.00–20.00 ❗ Admission charge

Hiking

The hour-long hike to the top of Monte de Santa Agueda, one of Menorca's highest hills, is well worth the effort, not so much for the ruined Moorish fort of Castell Santa Agueda at the top, but for the breathtaking island vistas and the incredible sense of history along the original Roman road that forms a section of the walk. To find the start of the walk, continue up the same road as for Binisues Museum House (see page 81) and, just before the tarmac stops, there is a clearing on the right-hand side to leave your car, with wooden signs indicating the route. It's hard-going in the height of summer.

SHOPPING

Castillo Menorca

This shopping complex between Ferreries and Ciutadella is a great port of call for all the family – there is an excellent range of souvenirs in the shop, and a pool, go-kart track and 1.6 ha (4 acres) of grass for children, plus a mini Indian reservation to run around in. The huge Lladró showroom here has one of the largest collections of porcelain figurines in Europe.

Ⓐ Carretera Maó–Ciutadella, Km 35 Ⓣ 971 26 91 24 Ⓦ www.castillomenorca.com Ⓛ 10.00–19.00 Mon–Sat

Artesania Maria Janer

Unusual and quality presents from pottery, wood, glass and paper.

Ⓐ Carrer De Sa Font 24 Ⓣ 971 37 40 02 Ⓛ 10.30–13.00 & 17.00–19.00

Los Claveles

This specialist bakery produces Menorcan biscuits and pastries.

Ⓐ Avinguda Verge del Toro 4 Ⓣ 971 37 31 28 Ⓛ 09.30–13.30 & 17.00–19.00

Shoes are a good buy in Ferreries. Try the huge **Jaime Mascaro** factory outlet, the **Ferrerias Centre** and **Industrial Artesanas Menorca** factory shop on the industrial estate on the outskirts of town.

TAKING A BREAK

Restaurants & bars

Bar Ca'n Bernat £ A busy locals' tapas bar with great views over the pretty town square right opposite the church. Try the local cured ham.

Ⓐ Plaça de l'Església Ⓣ 971 37 31 10 Ⓛ 08.00–23.00

Mesón Galicia £ This is a small, homely restaurant and tapas bar that serves a range of hearty meat and fish dishes from Galicia in northern

Spain. Well worth a visit. ⓐ Carretera Maó 15 ⓣ 971 37 38 83 ⓛ 19.30–23.00 Thur–Sun

Liorna ££ This gem of an elegant restaurant with a garden is hidden down a backstreet in the older part of town. The emphasis is on local produce, with wonderful seafood and pizzas on offer, and cocktails made from local Xoriguer gin (see page 96). ⓐ Carrer Econom Florit 9 ⓣ 971 37 39 12 ⓦ www.liorna.com ⓛ 19.00–23.00

Mesón El Gallo ££ Try one of the specialities – *parrillada* (mixed barbecued grill), steak with Mahón cheese or paella de Gallo – at this 200-year-old farmhouse restaurant. ⓐ Just outside Ferreries on the Carretera Cala Santa Galdana, Km 1.5 ⓣ 971 37 30 39 ⓛ 12.30–15.00 & 19.30–23.00 Tues–Sun

Binisues £££ A top-notch restaurant in elegant surroundings offering a wide range of quality dishes. The proprietor has his own fishing boats at Ciutadella, so the house specialities include the freshest of fish, shellfish and lobster casserole. ⓐ Camí dels Alocs, Carretera Maó–Ciutadella, Km 31.6 ⓣ 971 37 37 28 ⓛ 12.00–23.00 Mon–Sat

The rooftops of Ferreries

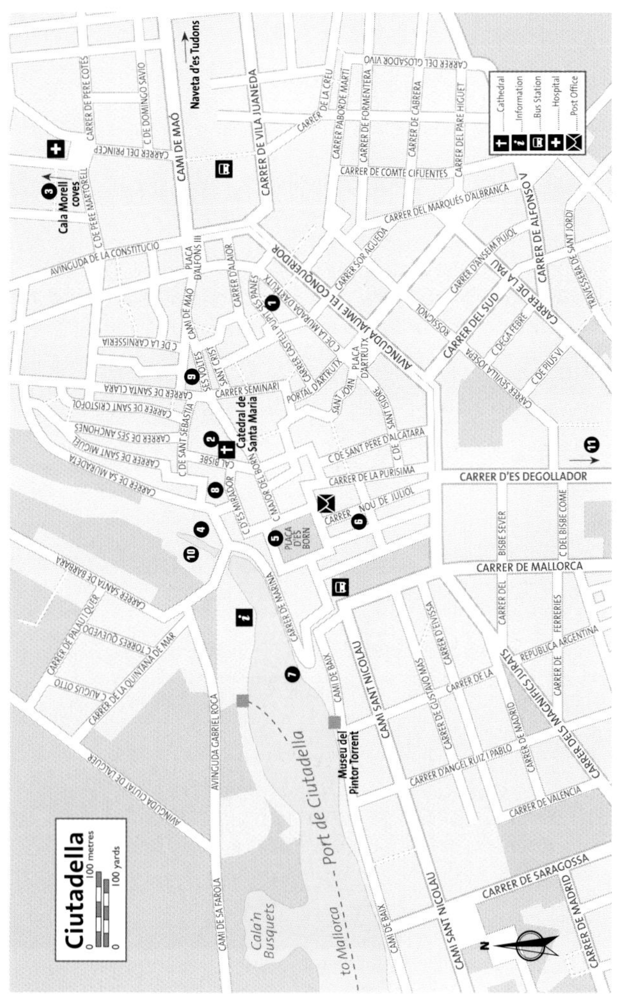
Ciutadella
0 100 metres
0 100 yards
Cathedral
Information
Bus Station
Hospital
Post Office
Naveta d'es Tudons
Cala Morell coves
Catedral de Santa Maria
Museu del Pintor Torrent
Port de Ciutadella
to Mallorca
Cala'n Busquets
Plaça d'es Born
Plaça d'Alfons III
Plaça d'Artrutx
Cami de Maó
Carrer de Vila Juaneda
Avinguda Jaume I el Conqueridor
Avinguda de la Constitució
Carrer del Sud
Carrer de la Pau
Carrer de Alfonso V
Carrer d'es Degollador
Carrer de Mallorca
Carrer dels Magnífics Jurats
Camí Sant Nicolau
Camí de Baix
Carrer de Marina
Carrer de Saragossa
Carrer de Madrid
Avinguda Gabriel Roca
Camí de Sa Farola
Avinguda Ciutat de l'Alguer
Carrer de Santa Bàrbara
Carrer de la Quintana de Mar
Carrer de Comte Cifuentes
Carrer del Marqués d'Albranca
Carrer Seminari
Ses Voltes
Portal d'Artrutx
Carrer Nou de Juliol
Carrer de la Purísima
C de Sant Pere d'Alcàtara
Carrer de Sa Muradeta
Carrer de Sant Miquel
Carrer de Ses Anchones
Carrer de Sant Cristòfol
Carrer de Santa Clara
C de Sant Sebastià
C Major del Born
C d'es Mirador
Carrer d'Alaior
Carrer del Princep
Carrer de Pere Cotes
C de Domingo Savio
Carrer Sor Agueda
Carrer d'Anselm Pujol
Travessera de Sant Jordi
Carrer de València
Carrer d'Angel Ruiz i Pablo
Carrer de Gustavo Mas
Carrer d'Eivissa
Carrer de Formentera
Carrer de Cabrera
Carrer del Pare Huguet
Carrer Pabordé Martí
Carrer del Glosador Vivo
Carrer de la Creu
C de Pius VI
C de Ga Febre
Carrer Sevilla Josepa
Carrer Bisbe Sever
C del Bisbe Come
Carrer del Ferreries
Carrer de República Argentina
C de la Carnisseria
Carrer Castell Rupit
C de la Murada d'Artrutx
Ses Panes
Sant Crist
Sant Joan
Sant Isidre
Rossiscol
Carrer de Palau i Quer
C Torres Quevedo
C Augusto Otto
N

Ciutadella

Nowhere else in Menorca feels quite as Spanish as Ciutadella (pronounced Suit-a-della). When the British moved the capital to Maó from Ciutadella in 1722, the bishop of Menorca and several noble families stayed behind, and their palaces still line the ancient streets today. The Plaça d'es Born, the old parade ground at the heart of the city, is one of the finest squares in Spain.

Stroll along the narrow streets of the old town, located between Plaça d'es Born and the Plaça de Ses Palmeres. Wander down any of the streets to peer into the courtyards of old mansions with balconies, stone archways and coats of arms above the doors. Artists and jewellers have set up workshops in the backstreets around the cathedral, side by side with upmarket boutiques selling designer clothes. Come in the early evening as the people of Ciutadella gather beneath the whitewashed arches of Ses Voltes, or stop at a bar in Plaça Nova to drink in the atmosphere of this fascinating city.

BEACHES

Ciutadella's beach is at Cala d'es Degollador, a short walk from the centre at the end of the Carrer de Marina. Most people head for the pocket-size beaches at Sa Caleta and Cala Santandría south of the city.

THINGS TO SEE & DO

Catedral de Santa Maria (St Mary's cathedral)

Ciutadella's Gothic cathedral was built on the site of a former mosque, and the old minaret has been turned into a belfry. At the time of writing it was under renovation although still open in part.

ⓐ Plaça de Sa Catedral ⓑ 10.00–14.00 Mon–Sat

Evening walk

The seafront promenade of Carrer de Marina, opened in 1997, is where the locals come to join in the evening ritual of the *paseo* (evening stroll).

The full walk, from the Plaça d'es Born to the small beach at Cala d'es Degollador, takes a leisurely half hour each way, and the views along the seafront are superb.

Museu del Pintor Torrent (José Roberto Torrent Museum)
A small exhibition by José Roberto Torrent, who painted magical scenes of Menorca and died in 1990.
ⓐ Carrer Sant Rafael 11 ◷ 11.00–13.00 & 19.30–21.30 (June–Oct); 17.00–21.00 Fri–Sat (Nov–May)

Naveta d'es Tudons (Burial chamber)
This Bronze Age burial chamber in the shape of an upturned boat was restored to its original condition in 1975.
ⓐ A dusty walk from the main road from Ciutadella to Maó, 4 km (2½ miles) from Ciutadella ◷ 09.00–20.00 Tues–Sat, 09.00–15.00 Sun & Mon

Plaça d'es Born (Born Square)
The Born is the meeting place of all Ciutadella; get there early in the evening to watch the world go by with a beer or coffee in one of the square's bars. From the old city walls on the north side there is a great view of the harbour at the end of the long, narrow creek.

EXCURSIONS

Cala Morell coves
Just 8 km (5 miles) away on the largely deserted northeast coast of the island, this small, exclusive resort is best known for the prehistoric caves in the cliffs that frame a picturesque cove and tiny pocket of sand. The swimming and snorkelling are excellent here, just as they are at the idyllic, sandy beaches of Algaiarens slightly to the east and reached by car.

Cruise the coast
Take a day trip by boat from Ciutadella Harbour to some of the island's most beautiful beaches of Cala Son Saura, Cala'n Turqueta and Cala

Ciutadella harbour is a good place to watch the sun set

Macarella on the south coast. Most companies include free paella and sangría in the price. Wander along the harbour to find them.

Hire a bike

Cycling is a great way to explore the city and the surrounding countryside.

Bicicletas Tolo, Carrer Sant Isidre 32 971 38 15 76 09.00–13.00 & 15.30–19.30 Mon–Fri, 09.00–13.00 Sat, 09.30–10.30 Sun

Mallorca

Mallorca is 75 minutes away from Ciutadella by fast boat, organised by the Cape Balear sailing company. There are between one and three daily sailings to Cala Ratjada in Mallorca.

Cape Balear, Moll Comercial 971 81 86 68

TAKING A BREAK

Restaurants & bars

Bar Ulises £ ❶ Join locals here for an early-morning coffee in the market square. ⓐ Plaça de la Llibertat ⓣ 971 38 00 31 ⓛ 06.00–15.30 & 18.00–22.00 Mon–Thur, 06.00–15.30 & 18.00–23.00 Fri, 06.00–15.00 Sat

Café Central £ ❷ A popular tapas bar right underneath the cathedral. ⓐ Plaça de Sa Catedral ⓣ 971 48 22 08 ⓛ 09.00–24.00 Mon–Fri, 09.00–15.00 Sat–Sun

Bar a l'Estiu ££ ❸ Clinging on to the cliffside in Cala Morell, this little bar has views across the minuscule beach, bathing platforms and sandy cliffs. Choose raciones of fab prawns and tasty tomato salad. It's the only place to eat near the beach and so gets very busy. ⓐ Cala Morell ⓛ 12.00–17.00

Ciutadella, Menorca's former capital

SHOPPING

The narrow streets of the old quarter are full of small, specialist shops. Try **Carrer Seminari** for art, jewellery and antiques, **Carrer de Sa Carnisseria** for clothes, and the central street, with its vast whitewashed arcades, usually known as Ses Voltes, for just about anything of quality. A good shoe shop is **Ca Sa Pollaca** (ⓐ Ses Voltes), which has been selling handmade leather shoes since 1897. **Ca n' Padet** (ⓐ Plaça Mercat) has a good selection of Menorcan cheeses, herbs, wines and spirits. The colourful daily market in **Plaça de la Llibertat** is a fun place to shop for fish and foodstuffs. Also worth a visit are:

Hiper Ciutadella Out-of-town hypermarket. On the road to Cala'n Bosch and a good place to pick up picnics. 🕒 09.00–21.00 Mon–Sat

Sa Gelateria de Menorca (ⓐ Costa d'es Moll) and **Gelateria Es Pins** (ⓐ Plaça d'es Pins). Both serve a dazzling choice of ice-cream flavours. 🕒 Both parlours 11.00–24.00 in season

Café Balear ££ ❹ By far the most popular restaurant by the harbour. There are a few tables by the quayside plus a few inside and a constant throng of hungry and well-heeled locals waiting to grab them. The seafood comes in daily on the owner's boat, the *Rosa Santa*. Book or get there early. ⓐ Es Pla de Sant Joan 15, Port de Ciutadella ⓣ 971 38 00 05 🕒 19.00–23.30

Cas Cònsol ££ ❺ Trendy bar and restaurant serving modern Mediterranean food, with views overlooking the harbour. There's a tiny terrace illuminated with fairy lights; perfect for a romantic supper. ⓐ Plaça des Born 17 ⓣ 971 48 46 54 🕒 12.00–16.00 & 19.00–01.00

Don Giacomo ££ ❻ Pizzas from a wood-fired oven and imaginative Mediterranean dishes, such as duck with pears, served in an old town-

house close to the main square. Bursting at the seams most weekends. Ⓐ Carrer Nou de Juliol 5 Ⓣ 971 38 32 79 Ⓛ 12.00–16.00 & 19.00–01.00

S'Arrosseria ££ ❼ A good-value place under awnings along the seafront serving paella and seafood. For a change of taste, try one of their crispy pizzas in a multitude of varieties. Ⓐ Port de Ciutadella 23 Ⓣ 971 48 17 35 Ⓦ www.recibaria.com Ⓛ 12.00–16.00 & 19.00–01.00

El Horno £££ ❽ A sophisticated French restaurant. Try the rabbit with red wine and mushrooms, or chicken in cream and tarragon sauce. Ⓐ Carrer d'es Forn 12 Ⓣ 971 38 07 67 Ⓛ 19.00–22.30

Es Puntet £££ ❾ One of the new breed of designer eateries opening up in Ciutadella. Simple and sleek interior with spectacular lighting and an equally spectacular menu with quality local cod, seafood and squid served simply. A good wine list with some Catalan examples. Ⓐ Ses Voltes 24 Ⓣ 971 48 48 63 Ⓛ 19.00–23.00 Mon–Sat

AFTER DARK

Bars & clubs

Lateral ££ ❿ The open space behind the fishing harbour is the setting for several late-night clubs and bars in old warehouses, of which this is great for late-night dancing with the locals. Ⓐ Es Pla de Sant Joan 9 Ⓛ 20.00–late (summer) ⓘ Closed winter

Pedros ££ ⓫ Disco playing the hits of the '70s, '80s and '90s in affluent little Cala Santandria. There is karaoke and live music on Friday and Saturday. Ⓐ Camí ses Vinyes, Cala Santandria Ⓣ 971 48 02 48 Ⓛ 20.00–02.00 June–Oct

▶ *Menorca has many fine views*

You can get any cuisine you like in Menorca

Food & drink

Restaurants in Menorca cater for a wide range of tastes – in the larger resorts you can get anything from an English breakfast to a Chinese takeaway. Traditional Menorcan cuisine, however, is typically Mediterranean, making full use of local products – especially seafood – and heavily flavoured with garlic, tomatoes and herbs. Recently, a series of boutique restaurants has sprung up in Ciutadella and Maó, where the high quality of food is matched by superb service and stylish interior design.

FISH & SEAFOOD

Local fish and seafood are always excellent – prawns and mussels feature on almost every menu, and squid, swordfish and sole are all widely available. Fish is sometimes baked in the oven with potatoes, tomatoes and breadcrumbs, but you can usually ask for it to be grilled. The most famous seafood dish of all is *caldereta de langosta*, a lobster casserole served in an earthenware bowl. You can eat this at restaurants all over the island, but the best place is definitely beside the harbour at Fornells (see pages 64–5).

MEATS

The Menorcans are hearty meat-eaters. Charcoal grills are a speciality, as are roast suckling pig and shoulder of lamb. Every bar has its own *jamón serrano*, a whole cured ham that is sliced into sandwiches or nibbled with pre-dinner drinks. The local *sobrassada* sausage, made by mincing raw pork with hot peppers, is delicious on toast or for tapas.

PAELLA

The classic Spanish dish is paella, a mound of steaming rice flavoured with saffron and topped with everything from mussels and prawns to pieces of chicken. Paella is available everywhere in Menorca, but be wary of anyone who says they can serve paella immediately – if cooked properly it takes at least 30 minutes to produce.

PIZZA

Pizza may not be a local dish, but the pizzas on Menorca are some of the best you will find anywhere. Most pizzerias cook them the Italian way, in a traditional wood-fired oven, with a thin, crispy base and toppings ranging from grilled vegetables to Mahón cheese.

TAPAS

These Spanish snacks are designed to whet the appetite before a meal, but order several portions and they make an interesting light lunch or supper in themselves. Tapas are lined up at the bar in metal trays, so it is easy to pick out what you want and point to it. Typical tapas include *pinchos* (kebabs), *calamari* (squid rings) and *albóndigas* (meatballs in tomato sauce), but two of the simplest are *tortilla*, a potato omelette, and *pa amb oli*, toast rubbed with tomato and garlic and sprinkled with olive oil.

DESSERTS

Most restaurants offer fresh fruit or ice cream – La Menorquina ice creams, which originated in Alaior, are popular throughout Spain. A popular local dessert is *crema Catalana*, a custard with a caramelised sugar topping. If you don't have a sweet tooth, ask for a plate of Mahón cheese, a strongly flavoured, hard cheese produced in Alaior (see pages 71 and 73).

WINE & BEER

The best Spanish wines come from Rioja, although reds and whites from the Penedés region are often better value, and Cava, or Spanish champagne, makes an inexpensive and special sparkling treat. *Cerveza* (beer) is usually lager, sold either bottled or draught – if you want draught, ask for *una caña*. Bars in the resorts have a wide selection of imported beers and lagers.

OTHER ALCOHOLIC DRINKS

Gin has been produced on Menorca for hundreds of years and the best comes from the Xoriguer distillery in Maó. Drink it neat or with tonic, but the classic Menorcan drink, always drunk at festivals, is *pomada*, which is gin with lemon. Most bars have a good array of Spanish brandies on display. Sangría is an alcoholic fruit punch based on brandy, red wine and lemonade – delicious, but much more potent than it tastes. Try sangría made with champagne.

SOFT DRINKS

The tap water is safe to drink but most people prefer mineral water – *agua con gas* is sparkling, *agua sin gas* is still. Popular drinks, such as Coca-Cola and lemonade, are available everywhere, and some bars offer freshly squeezed fruit juice or *granizado*, a fruit drink with crushed ice. The Spanish always ask for *café solo* after dinner – a small shot of strong, dark coffee like an espresso – but visitors should have no trouble ordering a *café con leche*, made with hot milk, or a *descafeinado*, decaffeinated coffee.

EATING OUT

The Spanish tend to eat very late. In the larger resorts it is possible to find food at any time of day, but in Maó, Ciutadella and the inland towns most restaurants do not open before 13.00 for lunch and 20.00 for dinner – most people come a lot later than this.

At lunchtime, many restaurants offer a *menú del día*, which is a three-course set meal, including wine or water, at a very good price. There is not usually a lot of choice, but the food is always filling, local and fresh and makes a good option.

Don't be afraid to try local restaurants – most have menus with English translations, and even if they do not, the waiter will usually be able to explain what's what.

Menu decoder

Aceitunas aliñadas Marinated olives

Albóndigas en salsa Meatballs in (usually tomato) sauce

Albóndigas de pescado Fish cakes

Allioli Garlic-flavoured mayonnaise served as an accompaniment to just about anything – a rice dish, vegetables, shellfish – or as a dip for bread

Bistek or **biftek** Beef steak; rare is *poco hecho*, *regular* is medium and *bien hecho* is well done

Bocadillo Sandwich, usually made with baguette

Caldereta Stew based on fish or lamb

Caldo Soup or broth

Carne Meat; *carne de cerdo* is pork; *carne de cordero* is lamb; *carne picada* is minced meat; *carne de ternera* is beef

Chorizo Cured, dry and spicy red sausage made from chopped pork, paprika, spices, herbs and garlic

Churros Flour fritters cooked in spiral shapes in very hot fat and cut into strips, best dunked into hot chocolate for breakfast

Cordero asado Roast lamb flavoured with lemon and white wine

Crema catalana Vanilla-flavoured custard with a burned-sugar topping

Embutidos charcuteria Pork meat preparations including *jamón* (ham), *chorizo* (see above), *salchichones* (sausages) and *morcillas* (black pudding)

Ensalada Salad – usually composed of lettuce, onion, tomato and olives

Ensalada mixta As above, but with extra ingredients, such as boiled egg, tuna fish or asparagus

Escabeche Sauce of fish, meat or vegetables cooked in wine and vinegar and served cold

Estofado de buey Beef stew, made with carrots and turnips, or with potatoes

Fiambre Any type of cold meat such as ham, chorizo, etc.

Flan Caramel custard, the national dessert of Spain

Fritura A fry-up, as in *fritura de pescado* – different kinds of fried fish

Gambas Prawns; *gambas a la plancha* are grilled, *gambas al ajillo* are fried with garlic and *gambas con gabardina* deep-fried in batter

Gazpacho andaluz Cold soup (originally from Andalucía) made from tomatoes, cucumbers, peppers, bread, garlic and olive oil

Gazpacho manchego Hot dish made with meat (chicken or rabbit) and unleavened bread (not to be confused with *gazpacho andaluz*)

Habas con jamón Broad beans fried with diced ham (sometimes with chopped hard-boiled egg and parsley)

Helado Ice cream

Jamón Ham; *jamón serrano* and *jamón iberico* (far more expensive) are dry cured; cooked ham is *jamón de york*

Langostinos a la plancha Large prawns grilled and served with vinaigrette or *allioli. Langostinos a la marinera* are cooked in white wine

Lenguado Sole, often served cooked with wine and mushrooms

Mariscos Shellfish

Menestra A dish of mixed vegetables cooked separately and combined before serving

Menú del día Set menu for the day at a fixed price; it may or may not include bread, wine and a dessert, but it doesn't usually include coffee

Paella Famous rice dish originally from Valencia but now made all over Spain; *paella Valenciana* has chicken and rabbit; *paella de mariscos* is made with seafood; *paella mixta* combines meat and seafood

Pan Bread; *pan de molde* is sliced white bread; *pan integral* is wholemeal bread

Pincho moruno Pork kebab – spicy chunks of pork on a skewer

Pisto Spanish version of ratatouille, made with tomato, peppers, onions, garlic, courgette and aubergines

Pollo al ajillo Chicken fried with garlic; *pollo a la cerveza* is cooked in beer; *pollo al chilindrón* is cooked with peppers, tomatoes and onions

Salpicón de mariscos Seafood salad

Sopa de ajo Delicious warming winter garlic soup thickened with bread, usually with a poached egg floating in it

Tarta helada Popular ice-cream cake served as dessert

Ternasco asado Roast lamb flavoured with lemon and white wine

Tortilla de patatas Classic omelette, also called *tortilla española*, made with potatoes, that can be eaten hot or cold

Zarzuela de pescado y mariscos Stew made with white fish and shellfish in a tomato, wine and saffron stock

Shopping

Every resort has at least one souvenir shop, but for the widest and best-quality choice of local crafts you should wander around the old hearts of Maó and Ciutadella. If you've hired a car, visit some of the factory shops strung out along the main road between the two towns. **Es Plans** (ⓐ Just outside Alaior) has a good selection of leather goods, pottery and jewellery, while **Castillo Menorca**, in a mock castle near Ferreries, has a **Lladró** porcelain shop as well as shoes, handbags, Mallorca pearls and lace. **Llonga Per Piel** (ⓐ On the new ring road around Ciutadella) has a wide choice of costume jewellery and leather goods.

Another good place for picking up bargains is at the weekly outdoor markets that tour the island's main towns. The best are in the **Plaça de S'Esplanada in Maó** (Tues and Sat mornings) and the **Plaça d'es Born in**

Browsing at a jewellery market stall

Ciutadella (Fri and Sat mornings). On Saturday mornings there is a craft and local produce market in Ferreries. Other markets can be found at **Es Castell** (Mon & Wed), **Sant Lluís** (Mon & Wed), **Es Migjorn Gran** (Wed), **Alaior** (Thur), **Es Mercadal** (Sun), **Es Migjorn Gran** (Wed) and fresh produce markets in **Maó** and **Ciutadella** (Mon–Sat morning).

SHOES

Menorcan leather is wonderfully soft, and many of the shoes sold with Italian designer labels were actually produced in Menorca. Shop around and you can pick up some real bargains. Anything by **Looky**, **Patricia**, **Torres**, **Pons Quintana** or **Jaime Mascaro** is likely to be good quality. All these have their own shops in Maó and Ciutadella; there are also massive Jaime Mascaro factory shops on the outskirts of Ferreries and Alaior. A Menorcan speciality is *abarcas*, traditional leather sandals made by stitching two pieces of cow hide on to a pneumatic sole. These are so popular that you can even buy pottery versions as souvenirs!

FOOD & DRINK

Mahón cheese, one of the best in Spain, makes a good souvenir to take home – it is sold in square loaves coated with yellow rind and comes in several varieties, from young to very mature. There are several cheese shops in Alaior, where it was originally made. Other good buys are almond biscuits, Spanish wine and brandy, and Xoriguer gin, sold in earthenware bottles across the island.

MAÓ AIRPORT

If you've left your shopping to the last minute, the airport has decent souvenir and jewellery shops and a well-stocked tax-paid shop selling alcohol, perfume and cigarettes. There is also a Jaime Mascaro shoe shop in the check-in hall. Visitors returning to other countries in the EU can take unlimited perfume and wine and any items bought in Menorcan shops – as long as you have kept the receipt to show that you have paid the tax. The airport is currently being extended but is functioning fairly well.

Children

Menorca is the perfect destination for a holiday with children. The locals adore youngsters and will make a fuss of them wherever you go – even in the smartest restaurants.

BEACHES

There are lots of child-friendly and Blue Flag beaches, with safe, shallow water, Red Cross posts and beach toys and ice creams for sale. Most beaches also have pedaloes for hire; some with water-chutes. Most of the resorts have adventure playgrounds, sometimes with toboggan slopes and waterslides, and there are plenty of children's clubs where your children are looked after during the day while you relax without having to worry about them.

BOAT TRIPS

Children love anything that moves. A boat tour around Maó Harbour (see page 23) or a cruise along the south coast from Cala Galdana (see page 51) can become a real adventure with children on board. Glass-bottomed catamaran trips around Maó Harbour allow children to glimpse life beneath the sea (tickets available at the information office on the harbour front; ⓐ Yellow Catamarans ⓣ 639 676 351; ⓐ Don Joan Catamarans ⓣ 971 350 778).

HORSE RIDING

Horse rides and tuition are available at Pony Club in Sant Tomàs (see page 47) or at Hort de Llucaitx Park near Fornells (see page 67). Another attraction for children is the equestrian show held at the Espectacle Eqüestre, which features carriage rides, horsemanship displays and donkey rides in the interval (ⓐ Carretera Cala Galdana km 0.5, Ferreries ⓣ 971 15 50 59 ⓛ Show starts 20.30 Wed & Sun, June–Sept). Son Martorellet also has riding displays on elegant black Menorcan horses (see page 108; ⓐ 1 km (⅔ mile) further down the road to Cala Galdana ⓛ Shows Tues & Thur), and children can be shown around the stables.

MINI-TRAIN

Tour the larger resorts on a mini-train – you will be able to find these at Punta Prima, Cala'n Porter, Son Bou, Cala Caldana, Cala'n Bosch and Cala'n Bruch.

WATERSPORTS

Menorca's top children's attractions are the Club San Jaime at Son Bou. With a swimming pool, a waterslide and an interlocking maze, there is enough here to keep children happy for hours (see page 43); Aquarock and Kartingrock at Cala'n Bosch (see page 55) and Los Delfines Aquapark near Ciutadella (see page 59).

THEME PARK

The Fun House at Cala'n Porter lets children have fun in the bouncy castle or playing table tennis and pool while parents enjoy a quiet beer or a cocktail (see page 38).

Capers in a canoe

Sports & activities

Menorca is the perfect place for a relaxing holiday – but if you are looking for an active holiday, there are plenty of opportunities. The calm, clear waters of Menorca's sheltered coves make excellent conditions for watersports, while the gentle countryside inland is ideal for walking, cycling and horse riding.

HORSE RIDING

The Camí de Cavalls is an ancient bridle path running around the coastline perfect for gentle hacks through the beautiful Menorcan countryside. Pony and horse hire, as well as riding lessons, are available from the following centres:

S'Hort de Llucaitx Park Trekking on ponies or horses (see page 67).

Stables Farm Novice and experienced, family and group rides. Try the ride down to the remote Cala Coves to see hidden Menorca. ⓐ Carretera Me-12 Cala'n Porter Sant Climent, Km 7.6 ⓣ 971 15 32 00 ⓛ 10.00–12.00 & 17.00–19.00

Pony Club Lessons and hacks (see page 47) ⓐ Parcela H9 s/n, Sant Tomàs ⓣ 676 68 85 78 ⓛ 10.00–12.00 & 17.00–19.00 Sat–Thur ⓘ Closed Fri

WALKING & CYCLING

Menorca Velo and Menorca Trekking, branches of **Club Activ** (ⓣ 971 37 38 43) organise excursions into Menorca's hidden countryside. Bike hire is also available in the larger resorts. There are cycling tracks around the island, passing ancient monuments and sheltered coves.

There are walks around the coastline to coves that cannot be reached by road. The 20-km (12-mile) historic Camí d'en Kane meanders from Maó to Es Mercadal and can be covered by bike or on foot, on horseback or by car.

WATERSPORTS

Sailing and windsurfing schools include **Surf'n'Sail Menorca at Son Xoriguer** (ⓣ 971 38 70 90), **Windsurf Fornells** at the entrance to

Fornells (t 971 18 81 50 e wfornells@excellence.es) and **Sports Massanet** in Ciutadella Harbour (t 971 48 21 86). All offer tuition to beginners and also hire out equipment.

The clear waters around Menorca's coves are ideal for snorkelling, but if you want to see more of the marine life and get inside some of the caves, try scuba diving. Courses for all are offered at **Dive Cala Blanca** (t 617 65 69 06 w www.divecalablanca.com), the **Diving Centre** in Fornells (t 971 37 64 31) and **S'Algar Diving and Aquasports** (t 971 15 06 01 w www.salgardiving.com). Remember that it is dangerous to fly within 24 hours of diving.

OTHER SPORTING ACTIVITIES

Bowls

Visit S'Algar Sports complex for seven greens (see page 30; t 971 35 94 54) and Bou Bowl in Son Bou (see page 43).

Cricket

The Menorca CC (Menorca Cricket Club) has a pitch at Biniparrell near Sant Lluís. There are fixtures throughout the summer months. t 971 15 08 07 w www.menorcacc.com

Golf

The 18-hole course at Son Parc (see page 66) is open to visitors booking in advance. a Urbanización Son Parc s/n t 971 35 90 59 w www.golfsonparc.com

Go-karting

Kartingrock has a 20,000 sq m (215,200 sq ft) track with single and double karts, so parents can ride with smaller children (see page 55). a Cala'n Bosch t 971 38 78 22 w www.aquarockmenorca.com

Tennis

Tennis courts are found in most larger resorts, and some major hotels also have facilities.

Streets adorned during the festa de Sant Cristòfol *in Es Migjorn Gran*

Festivals & events

CLASSICAL CONCERTS

Music is an ancient tradition in Menorca; the international music festival in Maó in July and August holds recitals at 21.30 in a variety of venues, including Santa Maria church. A similar festival is held in Ciutadella during the same months. The classical music festival in Fornells also runs through July and August, with concerts held on five Thursdays across that time. Local music and dancing displays can be found at weekends during the summer in main towns and major resorts. See local press and posters around town for details.

There are daily organ concerts between April and October at 11.30 every morning except Sunday in the church of Santa Maria in Maó. Recitals in Ciutadella are held at El Socors church at 11.30 Tues–Thur, June and September. The Teatro Principal in Maó was closed at the time of writing, as was the Teatre Principe in Ciutadella's Plaça d'es Born.

JAZZ

An international jazz festival takes place on Menorca in the summer months, with concerts and exhibitions held across the island. For details, see the local press, *Menorca magazine* or contact Menorca Jazz Obert (W www.jazzobert.com). To hear live jazz on a weekly basis, head to the Casino de Sant Climent, on the main street of Sant Climent, from 21.30 on Tuesdays (see page 34). Join in on the piano just up the road at Musupta Cusi's regular jamming sessions (see page 35).

LOCAL FESTIVALS

Every town in Menorca has its annual festival in honour of its patron saint, with street parties, parades of model giants, musical extravaganzas from folk dancing to pop groups, spectacular firework displays and testosterone-filled displays of horse riding in the main square – these are known as *jaleos*. Some of the largest festivals take place in Es Castell (Sant Jaume, 24–26 July), Ferreries (Sant Bartomeu, 23–25 August) and Maó (Fiesta de la Verge de Gràcia, 7–9 September), but the biggest and most colourful of all is the festival of Sant Joan (St John), held in Ciutadella on 23–24 June, when up to 150 horses and riders take part in the flamboyant *jaleo* – one at night and another at midday the following day. It begins with a swirling horse-back procession with the riders of jet-black Menorcan horses mingling with the crowds, and ends with a massive firework display in Plaça d'es Born, and in between are two days of riotous festivities, all fuelled by large amounts of *pomada* – gin with lemon (see page 97).

Calendar of local festivals

23–24 June	Sant Joan, Ciutadella
13–15 July	Sant Martí, Es Mercadal
20–22 July	Sant Antoni, Fornells
24–26 July	Sant Jaume, Es Castell
28–30 July	Sant Cristòfol, Es Migjorn Gran
11–13 Aug	Sant Llorenç, Alaior
18–20 Aug	Sant Climent, Sant Climent
23–25 Aug	Sant Bartomeu, Ferreries
24–26 Aug	Sant Lluís, Sant Lluís
7–9 Sept	La Verge de Gràcia, Maó

RIDING AND TROTTING

Son Martorellet, on the road from Ferreries to Cala Galdana, gives twice-weekly shows of Menorcan dressage on beautiful black horses (Tues & Thur, see page 102). There's a children's play area, bar and horse museum as well. The stables are open for visits every day except Sunday (ⓐ Carretera Cala Galdana km 1.7 ⓣ 609 049 493 ⓦ www.sonmartorellet.com).

The Menorcan passion for horses can also be seen at the trotting races that take place each weekend at the racetracks outside Maó and Ciutadella. There is a fun, family atmosphere and most people have a small bet on the horses. The races begin at around 18.00 in Maó on Saturdays and, in Ciutadella, at 18.00 on Sundays.

Cala Galdana

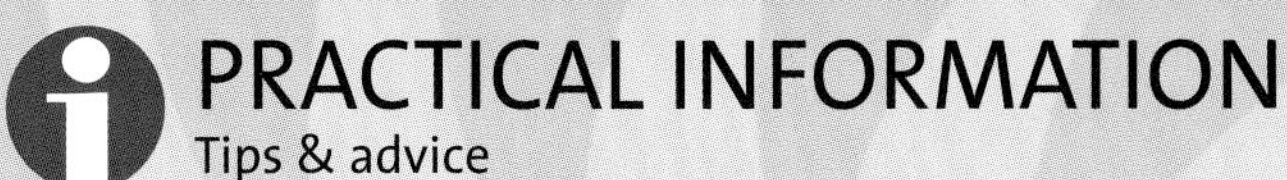
PRACTICAL INFORMATION
Tips & advice

Accommodation

HOTELS IN MENORCA

Menorca has a wide range of accommodation to suit all budgets and families, but finding accommodation as an independent traveller can be difficult as many hotels are contracted to travel companies.

Escape the crowds by booking into an agrotourism – a farmhouse or villa offering B&B accommodation in rural areas. These properties have charm and character and allow greater independence than hotels.

All prices are for a double room per night for two people and breakfast only and are peak season (July–Aug).

£ under 100 euros
££ 100–150 euros
£££ over 150 euros

Viva Menorca Apartments £ Five smart blocks surrounding a lagoon-shaped swimming pool. Self-catering is an option but the hotel has a restaurant with a pretty terrace. There's internet access, a sauna, and entertainment at the bar most nights. The rooms at the front of the hotel get a lot of traffic noise, so ask to be by the pool. ⓐ Calle Llevant s/n, Cala'n Bosch ⓣ 971 38 78 43 ⓦ www.hotelsviva.com

Sol Milanos Pingüinos £ The 600 three-star rooms are plainly furnished with balconies, most with a sea view. Good facilities for the whole family include a themed restaurant, children's club and nightly shows. ⓐ Platja de Son Bou, Alaior ⓣ 971 37 12 00 ⓦ www.solmelia.com

Cala Galdana Hotel & Villas d'Aljandar ££ Modern hotel and self-catering apartments in manicured grounds with a shady pool fringed with palms just two minutes from the sea. This is a good option for families with young teenagers as there are lots of cafés and snack bars within the complex and safe fun to be had on and around the beach. ⓐ Cala Galdana, Ferreries ⓣ 971 15 45 00 ⓦ www.hotelcalagaldana.com

Hotel Es Mercadal ££ A stylishly renovated traditional townhouse in the middle of sleepy Es Mercadal (see page 76). There are six smartly fitted bedrooms all with state-of-the-art en suites, a TV room, a little terrace bar and a tiled dining room. ⓐ Carrer Nou 49, Es Mercadal ⓣ 971 37 83 17

Hotel Sa Barrera ££ Lavishly Moroccan in theme, with ornate gilt ceilings and wrought ironwork. The terrace has a superb view of the little beach and a small pool to splash around in. ⓐ Calle Sa Barrera 12, Cala'n Porter ⓣ 971 37 71 26 ⓦ www.hotelsabarrera.com

Hotel Santo Tomàs ££ Sitting in neat gardens overlooking the sea and a great stretch of sandy beach, this modern hotel has a beauty centre, a library and both indoor and outdoor pools. Good for families with young children as the hotel backs straight on to the beach. ⓐ Platja de Sant Tomàs, Es Migjorn Gran ⓣ 971 37 00 25 ⓦ www.sethotels.com

Biniarroca Hotel Rural £££ Fifteenth-century whitewashed farmhouse with well-designed rooms. The property has an outdoor pool, verdant garden and a great restaurant open in the evenings. It's just the place for honeymooners. ⓐ Cami Vell 57, Sant Lluís ⓣ 971 15 00 59 ⓦ www.biniarroca.com

Hotel Port Ciutadella £££ A sleek urban choice overlooking the sea at Platja Gran. Rooms are ultra-modern, with spotless white bed linen and splashes of rich colour. The swimming pool is surrounded by decking, the spa is complete with sauna, steam bath, jacuzzi and massage treatments. ⓐ Passeig Marítim 36, Ciutadella ⓣ 971 48 25 20 ⓦ www.sethotels.com

Hotel Port Mahón £££ This elegant colonial-style hotel offers smart rooms with terraces and balconies as well as a swimming pool, late-night piano bar and sun terrace overlooking the sea. ⓐ Avinguda del Port de Maó, Maó ⓣ 971 36 26 00 ⓦ www.sethotels.com

Preparing to go

GETTING THERE

The cheapest way to get to Menorca is to book a package holiday with one of the leading tour operators specialising in Spanish island holidays. Package holidays are perfect for families who do not want the stress of organising their own flights, transport and accommodation. Food and drink at your chosen hotel often forms part of the deal. If your travelling times are flexible, and if you can avoid the school holidays, you can also find some very cheap last-minute deals using the websites for the leading holiday companies. Companies with particularly good facilities in Menorca include Thomas Cook (ⓦ www.thomascook.com), First Choice (ⓦ www.firstchoice.co.uk), Thomson Holidays (ⓦ www.thomson.co.uk) and the Holiday Warehouse (ⓦ www.holidaywarehouse.co.uk). Try ⓦ www.lastminute.com for cut-price last-minute deals on flights and accommodation.

By air

The majority of visitors use charter airlines to fly to Menorca, which operate from nearly all of the UK's regional airports. Carriers from outside the EU largely fly through Madrid or Barcelona on the Spanish mainland. Menorca's airport is being extended at the time of writing but is still functioning well. It is also served by scheduled international flights from the UK and by internal flights from Spanish airports at Madrid, Valencia and Barcelona.

ⓐ Maó airport ⓣ 971 36 3 0 92

British Airways flies scheduled to Maó from Gatwick (ⓦ www.britishairways.com).

easyJet flies scheduled from Bristol, Liverpool, Heathrow, Gatwick and Newcastle (ⓦ www.easyjet.com). First Choice flies charter flights from nine British airports including Bristol and Gatwick (ⓦ www.firstchoice.co.uk). Jet2 flies to Maó from Newcastle (ⓦ www.jet2.com). Monarch flies to Maó from Manchester, Birmingham, Luton and London Gatwick (ⓦ www.flymonarch.com). Thomson flies from Heathrow, Birmingham. Manchester, Cardiff and Edinburgh (W www.thomson.co.uk).

Many people are aware that air travel emits CO_2, which contributes to climate change. You may be interested in the possibility of lessening the environmental impact of your flight through the charity Climate Care, which offsets your CO_2 by funding environmental projects around the world. Visit W www.climatecare.org

By car and ferry

Few people choose to drive to Menorca from the UK, but it can be done. A two-day journey through France and Spain followed by an overnight ferry journey from either Barcelona or a weekly service (at the weekend) from Valencia run by Trasmediterranea, both arriving in Maó, does not make this a viable option for most families with children (W www.trasmediterranea.es).

TOURISM AUTHORITY

Further information about Menorca can be obtained from:

Spanish Tourist Office UK a 57–58 St James's Street, London W1A 6NB t 020 7486 8077/8034 W www.spain.info e tourspain@latestinfo.co.uk 09.15–13.30 Mon–Fri

Centre Port de Mao Consell Insular de Menorca a Moll de Llevant 2, Maó t 971 35 5 9 52 W www.e-menorca.org 09.30–19.00

Tourist Information Centre Ciutadella a Plaça de Sa Catedral 5 t 971 38 26 93 09.00–13.00 & 15.00–20.00

BEFORE YOU LEAVE

It is not necessary to have inoculations to travel in Europe, but you should make sure that you and your family are up to date with the basics, such as tetanus. It is a good idea to pack a small first-aid kit to carry with you containing plasters, antiseptic cream, travel sickness pills, insect repellent and/or bite-relief cream, antihistamine tablets, upset stomach remedies and painkillers. Sun lotion can be more expensive in Menorca so it is worth taking a good selection, especially of the higher-factor lotions if you have children with you. If you are taking prescription medicines, ensure that you take enough for the duration of your visit – you may find it difficult to obtain the same medicines in Menorca, although the staff in the pharmacies are trained to diagnose ailments and hand out medicines.

Check that your travel insurance policy covers you adequately for loss of possessions and valuables, for activities you might want to try – such as scuba-diving, horse riding or watersports – and for emergency medical and dental treatment, including flights home if required. Take an EHIC card form (available from post offices), which allows UK visitors access to reduced cost and sometimes free state-provided medical treatment in the European Economic Area (EEA). For further information, ring EHIC enquiries line (t 0845 605 0707) or visit the Department of Health website (w www.dh.gov.uk).

If you have medical insurance or are willing to pay, you can contact the private Salus Health Clinic (t freephone 900 60 50 50). The lines are open 24 hours a day and the staff speak English. Dental treatment is not usually covered by insurance, but in an emergency contact the Salus health clinic on the same number.

ENTRY FORMALITIES

Visitors from EU countries, including the United Kingdom and the Republic of Ireland, need a valid passport or national identity card. Visitors from Canada, the USA, Australia and New Zealand (among other countries) need a valid passport and may remain in Spain for a maximum period of 90 days without a visa. Citizens of most other countries, including South Africa, must apply for a visa at the nearest embassy or consulate before travelling to Spain. These regulations are subject to change and you should always check with the Spanish authorities before travel.

EU residents may carry any quantity of tobacco goods and alcohol which can be deemed to be for 'personal use' when travelling within the EU. Visitors to Spain from non-EU countries (if over 18) may bring 200 cigarettes, or 100 cheroots, or 50 cigars, or 250 grams of rolling tobacco, plus one litre of drink (over 22 per cent alcohol by volume), or two litres (under 22 per cent alcohol by volume). Perfumes are limited to 50 grams of perfume and 0.25 litres of eau de toilette.

MONEY

The currency in Menorca is the euro (€). The euro is divided into 100 cents, with coins of 1 and 2 euros and 1, 2, 5, 10, 20 and 50 cents. The note denominations are 500, 200, 100, 50, 20, 10 and 5 euros.

You will find cash dispensers in all the resorts and at the airport. Not many people use traveller's cheques any more (especially if travelling within Europe), but they are a safe way to carry money because it will be refunded if the cheques are lost or stolen. Most Menorcan outlets require you to use your PIN (personal identification number) when making a credit card purchase. You will also often be asked for a photographic form of ID.

CLIMATE

July and August can be very hot so check that your accommodation is air-conditioned when booking. May, September and October are warm without being too hot and there are fewer visitors than over the school holiday season. The Tramontana wind blows over the north of the island, bringing variable and sometimes wet weather in the early winter.

BAGGAGE ALLOWANCE

Baggage allowances vary according to the airline, destination and the class of travel, but 20 kg (44 lb) per person is the norm for luggage carried in the hold. You are also allowed one item of cabin baggage weighing up to 10 kg (22 lb) and measuring roughly 55 by 40 by 20 cm (22 by 16 by 8 in). Check with your airline as hand baggage allowances continue to change. In addition, you can usually carry duty-free purchases, umbrella, handbag, coat, camera, laptop, etc. as hand baggage. Surfboards, golf clubs, collapsible wheelchairs and pushchairs are usually charged as extras on charter flights and it is a good idea to let the airline know in advance that you want to bring these.

During your stay

AIRPORT

Menorca's only airport is 5km (3 miles) from Maó. The airport is currently being extended but all facilities are still open. There are plenty of food and drink outlets but queues can be long. There are a number of airport shops selling products from alcohol, cigarettes and perfume to locally produced goods such as shoes, cheese and jewellery.

Taxis

There are taxis outside arrivals that will take you anywhere across the island. They should be metered.

Car hire

Car hire is available from the arrivals hall – all the major car rental companies are represented, although it is cheaper to arrange hire over the internet before leaving home (see page 120 for details).

TELEPHONING MENORCA FROM ABROAD

Dial 00 (international dialling code), 971 (the Balearic Islands local code) and the six-digit number.

TELEPHONING ABROAD

Australia: 00 + 61 + area code (minus the 0) + telephone number
New Zealand: 00 64 + area code (minus the 0) + telephone number
Republic of Ireland: 00 353 + area code (minus the 0) + telephone number
South Africa: 00 27 + area code (minus the 0) + telephone number
UK: 00 44 + area code (minus the 0) + telephone number
United States and Canada: 00 1 + area code (minus the 0) + telephone number

COMMUNICATIONS

Postal services

Many shops selling postcards will have stamps too. Opening hours of the main post offices, or *Correos*, are:

ⓐ Maó ⓑ 09.00-21.00 Mon–Fri, 09.00–14.00 Sat

ⓐ Ciutadella ⓑ 09.00–19.00 Mon–Fri, Sat 09.00–14.00

Post offices in other towns may have odd opening hours but will largely follow the ones given above.

Telephones and internet access

Phone kiosks are everywhere, with instructions in several languages. Phonecards are available in post offices and shops for €6 or €12. You can also use your credit card in most public phones. A few bars and kiosks have metered phones where you can make your call first and pay for it afterwards. Local calls are very cheap.

A few cafés in Maó and Ciutadella have internet access, as do several in the larger resorts. Most large hotels will have WiFi connections or some form of internet access.

Café I Gelats Parpal

A bar-café incorporating an internet café called World Next Door.

ⓐ Carrer Hannover 21, Maó ⓣ 971 35 34 75 ⓑ 11.00–22.00

Tobogán

Buzzing pizzeria with internet access.

ⓐ Platja Cala Galdana, Cala Galdana ⓣ 971 15 46 16 ⓑ 09.30–23.30

Viva Menorca Apartments

Internet access.

ⓐ Calle Llevant s/n, Cala'n Bosch ⓣ 971 38 78 43 ⓑ 24 hours

CUSTOMS

The Menorcans tend to dress up when they go out to eat or make their evening *paseo* along the streets of Maó and around the harbour in

Ciutadella. Lunch can be a long, lingering affair that can carry on until evening at the weekend. Dinner is usually a lighter affair that kicks off late at night, often not until 22.00. They survive this regime by taking a siesta each afternoon somewhere between 14.00 and 18.00 and filling up on tapas in the early evening. All shops, businesses and most bars and restaurants away from the tourist areas will close during the afternoon break. Although most locals will drink (mostly wine) with food, excessive imbibing is frowned upon.

DRESS CODES

Menorcans are Catholic, and will be offended by beachwear worn in the towns. Cover up when leaving the beach and do not wear skimpy shorts and tops when going into town. Men should never wander the streets in any town or resort without a T-shirt on. Beach dress is fine, however, for the more anglicised holiday resorts such as Cala'n Porter and Cala'n Bosch.

ELECTRICITY

Menorca has the same voltage (220 V) as the UK, but with small, round two-pin plugs, so you will need to bring an adaptor. These are readily available in the UK at electrical shops or major chemists. If you buy electrical appliances to take home, check that they will work in the UK.

EMERGENCIES

Medical services

The Spanish healthcare system is good. Most hospitals are modern and well equipped and the doctors and paediatricians are skilled. Remember to carry your EHIC card with you at all times and present it. Do not assume that they will speak much English outside resort areas, Maó and Ciutadella.

Salus has English-speaking doctors located across Menorca and provides a free 24-hour emergency helpline (900 71 17 11). In some areas, there will be someone providing a voluntary translation service to help with doctor's appointments.

EMERGENCIES

Pan-European emergency number: calls to 112 are free from any telephone (mobile/cellular or fixed line). The operator will put you in contact with the emergency service that you require.
Calls from SOS phones on the main roads are free.
Ambulance Service (Ambulancia) 061
Local Police (Policía Municipal, for reporting theft or lost items) 092
Guardia Civil (for major crime) 062
Fire Service (Bomberos) 085
Sea Rescue (Salvamento marítimo) 900 202 202

www.balearics.angloinfo.com is a useful website that has lists of English-speaking doctors and dentists in Menorca.

Consulates

The Honorary British Vice-Consul is based at:
Sa Casa Nova, Camí de Biniatap 30, 07720 Es Castell 971 36 33 73/971 35 46 90.

GETTING AROUND

By car

Like the rest of Spain, Menorca drives on the right. The speed limits are 90 km/h (55 mph) on the main highway, 50 km/h (30 mph) in towns and 30 km/h (20 mph) on country roads, unless otherwise indicated. These limits are strictly enforced, with frequent road-side speed traps, as are the drink-driving laws. Alcohol levels must not exceed 0.5 g/l in the bloodstream (0.25 mg/l in exhaled air). Children must sit in the back, and children under three must be strapped into a car seat – tell the hire firm if you need one (some firms charge extra for this). Seat belts must be worn at all times.

Talking on mobiles while driving is prohibited unless you have a hands-free service. If you break down, put on the reflective jacket before getting out of the car on the road and immediately deploy the warning triangle. Check that jacket and triangle are both in your hire car before departure.

There are several petrol stations around Maó and Ciutadella, and along the main road between the two, but there are few on the rest of the island so keep the tank topped up. Most petrol stations are open 07.00–21.00 and a few are open for 24 hours. Most of the others have self-service machines outside these hours where you can pay for your petrol in advance using euro notes or credit cards. All hire cars take the unleaded (*sin plomo*) petrol Eurosuper.

Useful words for drivers

aparcamiento parking
estacionamiento prohibido no parking
ceda al paso give way to the right and left
circunvalación ring road

Car hire

Public transport is pretty limited in Menorca (see opposite) so you may want to hire a car. To do so, you will need both parts of your UK driving licence with you. Most car hire companies accept a regular driver's licence if you're from the EU, US, Canada, Australia or New Zealand. If you are coming from outside these areas or from Iceland, Norway, Switzerland and Liechtenstein, you will need an International Driver's Licence.

You have to be 21 to hire a car and a credit card imprint is required when picking up the car. If you want more than one driver for the car, the other drivers must have their licences too.

There are car hire offices in all the main resorts and at the airport in the arrivals hall – the biggest local company is **Betacar** (ⓐ Maó airport ⓣ 971 36 64 00; ⓐ Conquistador 59, Ciutadella ⓣ 971 38 29 98).

Most major car rental companies also operate out of the airport, including **Alamo** (ⓦ www.alamo.co.uk), **Budget** (ⓦ www.budget.co.uk; www.easycar.com) and **Sixt** (ⓦ www.sixt.co.uk).

Public transport

From the bus station in Maó, buses run six times daily along the main road from Maó to Ciutadella. There are also bus services from Maó to Es Castell, Sant Lluís, Binibeca, Es Canutells, Cala'n Porter, Son Bou, Cala Galdana, Arenal d'en Castell, Son Parc and Fornells, and from Ciutadella to Cala Galdana, Cala'n Bosch, Sa Caleta and Cala'n Forcat. There are regular services between Maó and the airport and back again.

Taxis

Taxis are available in all of the main resorts. The taxis are not metered, so you should check the fare in advance. Drivers keep a list of fares for the most common routes and you can ask to see this. A tip of a couple of euros is always welcome!

HEALTH, SAFETY & CRIME

Health

People who are not used to the sun burn easily – and children are especially vulnerable. Cover up with a strong sunblock, wear a hat and keep out of the midday sun. In a hot climate you also need to drink a lot more fluids. Take a beach tent for toddlers to shelter from the sun.

The tap water is safe to drink in Menorca but can be very salty. Mineral water is widely available and cheap.

Easily recognised by the big green cross above the door with the word 'Farmacia', chemists on the island are very good. The staff are helpful and knowledgeable. There is always an emergency chemist open 24 hours (*farmacias de guardia*), and a list of the open chemists is posted in the window of all chemists.

Safety

In summer, the most popular beaches usually have lifeguards on duty and/or a flag safety system:

- Red (or black): dangerous – no swimming
- Yellow: good swimmers only – apply caution
- Green (or white): safe bathing conditions for all.

Never swim after drinking alcohol or when a red flag is flying. More remote beaches, such as Cala'n Turqueta and Cala Macarella, may be safe for swimming but there are unlikely to be lifeguards or life-saving amenities available. Some beaches have strong currents and you should exercise caution when swimming.

Crime levels in Menorca are low, although it is sensible to take precautions against pickpockets and bag snatchers in the crowded streets of Maó and Ciutadella. Don't carry money, wallets or passports in your back pockets and carry cameras and handbags slung across your body. Never leave valuables on view in your hire car and always, always lock the car. Adhere to speed limits and never take risks when parking – you will get a ticket for being even five minutes late back to the car.

Lost property

If you are unfortunate enough to fall victim to a rare crime, your insurance company will require you to go to the local police to report anything valuable that has been lost or stolen. The police dress in khaki and are normally pretty helpful, but most of them seem to be out on the roads catching speeding locals! Keep the original version and photocopies of any official forms or documents the police require you to fill out and sign.

MEDIA

A good selection of English newspapers can be bought in the resorts, the more popular ones being printed in Spain. Many popular English magazines can be easily found. The larger supermarkets have an excellent selection of newspapers and magazines for all ages. Most hotels have satellite TV so you can watch your favourite programmes in English. Most British-owned bars and restaurants also have satellite TV and usually organise a special night if there is an important event on TV.

OPENING HOURS

Banks: 08.30–14.15 Mon–Fri

Shops: 09.30–13.30, 17.30–20.30 Mon–Fri, 09.30–13.30 Sat. These times

are for shops in towns. Local shops in resorts may open all day – consult individual shops for opening times.
Supermarkets: 09.00–21.00 Mon–Sat, 09.00–14.00 Sun (however, not all supermarkets are open on Sunday).

RELIGION

The main religion in Menorca is Catholicism. All towns have at least one Roman Catholic church. The times of services and Mass are usually posted on the door.
ⓐ The Anglican Church, Santa Margarita, Calle Stuart, Es Castell
Ⓛ Services 09.00, 11.00 Sun, 11.00 Wed & Fri (healing service).
For services in Ciutadella contact the chaplain (ⓣ 971 35 23 78).
ⓐ The Evangelical Church, Es Castell Ⓛ Service 11.30 Sun
ⓐ The Evangelical Church, Maó Ⓛ Services 10.00, 18.00 Sun

TIME DIFFERENCE

Add or substract the given number of hours to or from Spanish time to get the time in each country
Australia + 8 (West) to 10 hours (East)
New Zealand + 10 hours
United Kingdom – 1 hour
United States – 6 (East) to 9 hours (Pacific)

TIPPING

A service charge of 10 per cent is normally added to restaurant bills, but a tip of an additional 5 to 10 per cent can be left at your discretion. If you are having a drink in a bar, leave some loose change. Up to 10 per cent is acceptable as a tip for taxi drivers, and a tour guide should be tipped at your discretion.

TOILETS

There are no public toilets in towns except in bars. It is normal to use these without purchasing anything although it is considered polite to buy something.

TRAVELLERS WITH DISABILITIES

On the whole Menorca is a disability-friendly island with easy access to most facilities, and most pavements are adapted for wheelchairs. Some beaches have good access but may not have toilet facilities nearby. There are taxis for wheelchair users but you must request these.

ACKNOWLEDGEMENTS

We would like to thank all the photographers, picture libraries and organisations for the loan of the photographs reproduced in this book, to whom copyright in the photograph belongs:
Pictures Colour Library Ltd (page 53);
Thomas Cook Tour Operations Ltd (pages 1, 8, 10, 13, 16, 28, 31, 32, 40–41, 42, 46, 57, 58,64, 67, 69, 89, 90, 94, 100, 103)
Eugenia/morgueFile (page 93)
Tracy Newton (pages 5, 109)
Wikimedia Commons (pages 20, 25)
World Pictures/Photoshot (pages 17, 35, 72, 75, 79, 80, 85, 106)

We would also like to thank the following for their contribution to this series:
John Woodcock (map and symbols artwork);
Becky Alexander, Patricia Baker, Sophie Bevan, Judith Chamberlain-Webber, Stephanie Evans, Nicky Gyopari, Krystyna Mayer, Robin Pridy (editorial support);
Christine Engert, Suzie Johanson, Richard Lloyd, Richard Peters, Alistair Plumb, Jane Prior, Barbara Theisen, Ginny Zeal, Barbara Zuñiga (design support).

Project editor: Diane Teillol
Layout: Donna Pedley
Copy editor: Joanne Osborn
Proofreader: Jan McCann
Indexer: Marie Lorimer

Send your thoughts to
books@thomascook.com

- **Found a beach bar, peaceful stretch of sand or must-see sight that we don't feature?**
- **Like to tip us off about any information that needs a little updating?**
- **Want to tell us what you love about this handy little guidebook and more importantly how we can make it even handier?**

Then here's your chance to tell all! Send us ideas, discoveries and recommendations today and then look out for your valuable input in the next edition of this title.

Email to the above address or write to:
HotSpots Series Editor, Thomas Cook Publishing, PO Box 227, Coningsby Road, Peterborough PE3 8SB, UK.